Make Money with Your Studio

Setting up and operating a successful recording studio

By Tom Volinchak

ISBN 0-634-06230-1

HAL•LEONARD® CORPORATION

7777 W. BLUEMOUND RD. P.O. BOX 13819 MILWAUKEE, WI 53213

Visit Hal Leonard Online at
www.halleonard.com

In Australia Contact:
Hal Leonard Australia Pty. Ltd.
22 Taunton Drive P.O. Box 5130
Cheltenham East, 3192 Victoria, Australia
Email: ausadmin@halleonard.com

Table of Contents

Introduction v

Chapter 1: A New Way of Thinking.......................................1
  A. You Are Your Studio's Biggest Asset!
  B. Expect and Plan for Failure
  C. Learn When and Why to Say "No"
  D. Walk the Walk
  E. Get Over Yourself!
  F. Success Is a Process, Not an Event

Chapter 2: Sales Techniques 9
  A. Speak the Universal Language of Images
  B. Speak in Terms of Features and Benefits
  C. Be a Great Listener and Take Notes
  D. Develop and Implement the Client Profile Sheet
  E. Proposals and Follow-ups
  F. Closing the Deal

Chapter 3: Marketing Techniques 21
  A. Business Cards
  B. Memorable Graphics
  C. Promotion
  D. Shameless Self-Promotion: Free Press / PR

Chapter 4: Your Business Toolbox 33
  A. Paperwork and Systems
  B. MONEY, MONEY, MONEY, MONEY, MONEY!
  C. Promotional Tools

Chapter 5: Adding Value to Your Business 53
  A. Creature Comforts
  B. Artist Comforts
  C. Music Industry Information
  D. Client Performances
  E. Post-Production Services
  F. Encoding
  G. Publishing
  H. Music Licensing

Chapter 6: Finding New Business 61

    A.   Diversify!

    B.   The Karaoke / Novelty Market

    C.   Record Stores

    D.   Bridal Shops and Wedding Planner Services

    E.   Charitable Compilations

    F.   Bumper Tunes and Theme Songs

    G.   Songwriter Organizations

    H.   Graphic Illustrators

    I.   Trade Shows

    J.   Commercials

    K.   Recorded Evidence

Chapter 7: The Demo 67

    A.   A Smart Layout

    B.   Sample Demo Layout

Chapter 8: A Word About Equipment 71

    A.   Essential Things to Consider

    B.   Approaches to Equipment

    C.   Hot Equipment Tips

Chapter 9: Studio Profiles..81

    A.   Tuneman Productions

    B.   Big Red Studios

    C.   Karma Recording Studio

    D.   A Sharp Recording Studio

Chapter 10: Resources 89

    A.   Educational Resources

    B.   Overcoming Roadblocks: How to Avoid Being Your Own Worst Enemy

    C.   Seminars

A Closing Note..97

About the Author..97

This book is dedicated
to my parents
who oftentimes went without
so that I could enjoy
the wonderful gift of music.

❖❖❖

Special thanks to my good friend
Susan Nanfeldt, an author herself,
who helped me focus and edit this book.

Introduction

For fourteen years of my life, I worked in the sales and marketing of high-tech industrial water processing technology. During the eighties and early nineties, I built upon my formal education (a B.S. in biology and graduate studies for an MBA) by spending a lot of time studying and emulating those who were the most successful in my industry. I attended seminars of great motivational speakers like Tony Robbins and Zig Ziegler, went through numerous sales and marketing training courses, and read more books on the subject of how to be successful than I care to remember.

Throughout that part of my life, I spent a lot of time daydreaming about music—about playing it, writing it, recording it, and about hopefully one day earning a living from it. Eventually, I rose to the level of National Product Manager for a major U.S. corporation; but despite that success, I wasn't happy. The music industry called out to me more and more each day, as the creative, artistic side of my brain starved.

Somewhere around 1990, I decided it was time to take all my playing, recording, and writing skills and somehow make a name for myself in the music industry. I had been very active in songwriter issues through my membership in the Nashville Songwriters Association (NSAI), and my familiarity with the group's policies led me to accept a position as a regional workshop coordinator. During the same period, I started freelance writing about musical issues that were important to me, built a little home studio, and started producing records. A short time later, I moved to Nashville and went to work for BMI as a licensing executive.

When I made the move to Nashville, I thought for sure I had reached heaven. Can you imagine? I was young enough to start a second career, and blessed with the ability to surround myself with people who were just like me: artists, musicians, producers, engineers, and dreamers. Finally, I found myself in an environment where people thought and spoke the same way that I did. Home at last! The first part of my self-prophecy was true because from the moment I arrived in Nashville, I immediately started meeting people in the music business, and readily found new musical activities to soothe my need for a music fix.

It should have made me happy, but restless fool that I am, it didn't. It seems that while I was appeasing the right side of my brain (the creative side), I was ignoring the part of me that understood and enjoyed the business world. I watched countless artists, producers, engineers, and musicians make bad business decisions, and I grew frustrated with the entire mess.

Throughout my years in the water industry, I had successfully put sales and marketing plans into action that made faceless executives and stockholders wealthy. I opened new territories and marketplaces, and provided leadership to my fellow employees. I knew how to make a business run successfully, and I wanted to feel that thrill again. So, in 1996, I decided to combine my knowledge of the business world with my love for music, and went into business for myself.

I found my niche in the music industry. The more I was exposed to artists, producers, engineers, and studio owners, the more I came to realize that, while they may be brilliant musically, artists lack the same kind of creativity, intuition, and know-how to find success in the industry that they love. Luckily, I had worked both sides of the fence, and combining the two was natural for me.

Therefore, my sole intent with this book is to help you, the creative talent, abandon a lot of self-restrictive thinking that can absolutely stop your budding career dead in its tracks. I'm hoping that you'll put some of these simple, straightforward techniques into practice, and open new doors to career success. I also hope that as you digest the concepts in this book, you will achieve a higher level of confidence and self-realization that will propel you toward all of your musical dreams.

chapter 1

A New Way of Thinking

The Important Issues You Will Deal with on the Road to Recording Success

From the very beginning of my music career, I was amazed to learn that aspiring artists and recordists frequently start their careers by accepting misconceptions and self-limiting notions that impede their paths to success. I want to help you recognize these pitfalls by eliminating them from your thought process so that you can focus on activities that will feed your efforts, instead of those that will detract from success.

The most important step you can take in growing your career is to adopt new, positive ways of thinking, and to present yourself as the professional that you are. Each of the six sections in this chapter will explode a common detrimental myth, and then address the issues that are essential to developing the new you.

A You Are Your Studio's Biggest Asset!

This is the most important point in this chapter: *There is no correlation between how much equipment you have and how successful you can be.*

It is vitally important to remember that music is not about technology; it is about creativity, passion, romance, hopes, and dreams. When an aspiring artist considers your studio and services, 99% of the time he does not care if you use an AKG C3000 or a Neumann U87. He is more than likely looking for someone who will work with him and listen to his specific needs.

As studio owners, we spend too much time worrying about all the high-tech equipment we cannot afford, and sometimes create a self-imposed mental block, which prevents us from finding and winning new business. We spend hours reading industry magazines and boning up on all the newest technology, not realizing that artists seldom care about all of this stuff; they just want successful recordings.

When I opened my first studio, I utilized a single Roland VS-1680 along with some modest outboard gear. In the first few weeks of operation, either I was blessed with projects that were simple guitar/vocal songwriter demos, or sequencer-based hip-hop projects that I could record a track at a time. Everything in my studio world was buzzing along nicely.

The first challenge of my ability to sell myself came when a local four-piece rock band walked into the studio looking to record a full-blown CD. Although they were not familiar with multi-track recording techniques, they were very tight, polished, and cognizant of the sound they wanted. I was comfortable that I could capture their essence with sixteen tracks, but apprehensive about recording an entire band, since my equipment limited me to eight inputs and therefore the ability to record only a maximum of eight tracks simultaneously.

The band wanted to lay foundation tracks with everyone playing at once. Since I routinely used seven mics to record the drums, the limitations of my equipment required that I either:

a) Use fewer drum mics and compromise in that area;

b) Tell the band that they would be better served at a competitor's facility that offered more inputs and tracks;

c) Be creative, sell myself, and come up with an effective solution.

My initial reaction was panic. I needed the work, but at the same time, I was tentative about pushing the capabilities of my equipment to its absolute limit. Finally, I concluded that not only did I have every piece of equipment required to make a nice record for these guys, but also had some really great production ideas that could take their performance to an even higher level than they were hoping for. I decided to book the job and go for the gusto.

My plan was straightforward and simple, and although somewhat unconventional, I designed it to yield nice results. I decided to record the entire band at once, isolating the drums to a separate sound booth. I used seven mics, and made sure that on the initial recording, I got keeper drum tracks. The rest of the instruments were recorded in a different iso-booth, and the vocalists in yet another. Overall, I used another six mics to capture the bass, rhythm guitar, lead guitar, and scratch vocals. I used a small Mackie mixer to combine these six signals and blend them into one decent-sounding track that I could use as a guide to multi-track the rest of the band at a later session. My ace in the hole on this project was the built-in click track on the Roland VS-1680, which allowed me to keep the band in sync without having to tie up a track for that task.

I was sweating bullets wondering how it would sound, and worrying whether the band would comment about my unconventional procedure. But I am happy to say that the initial recording went fine, and the subsequent overdubs worked famously. The record was one of the nicer ones I did in that studio.

The important lesson here is not my brilliance or ingenuity, because, in all honesty, this was simply a case of necessity being the mother of invention. What it does illustrate, however, is that the band chose me to record their project because they trusted me to make them sound good. At the end of the project, even though I didn't have all the fancy equipment that I originally thought I could not live without, the customer was delighted.

In your own studio adventures, it is crucial to remember that there are no right or wrong ways of recording anything. Each studio has strengths and limitations, and there is nothing unprofessional about finding your own way to get the job done. Focus on your assets rather than your limitations, concentrate on what you as a studio owner can do to make your clients happy, and you will find your horizons broadening and your list of satisfied customers growing. More importantly, you will grow in confidence, and those around you will begin recognizing you as the expert—regardless of how well you stock your studio.

Expect and Plan for Failure

I don't care how much money you invest into your studio, you are going to experience failures, equipment disappointments, and outright mistakes. You have to accept snafus and keep moving ahead. What makes studio failures extremely difficult to handle is that clients put a lot of faith in us—so much so, that they actually place the fate of their musical dreams in our hands. We tend to be so artistically in-line with our clients that when we do goof up, we take setbacks very seriously—sometimes so seriously that it can prevent us from continuing with a positive attitude about our abilities.

One of the most effective ways I have of dealing with day-to-day studio failures is to realize that a failure, no matter how big, is merely a single, isolated event. A failure on Monday is no indication that the same thing will happen on Tuesday. Rather than worrying about possible screw-ups and beating yourself up, it is better to convince yourself ahead of time that goof-ups *are* going to happen, and then condition yourself to calmly and honestly face your clients when those bumps in the road do occur. Adapt! Focus on how you are going to get back to the project game plan, and then move forward.

There are precautions you can take ahead of time to minimize the impact that any errors will have on your attitude, and subsequently, your livelihood. Here are a few things that have worked nicely for me over the years:

1. Tom's Immutable Rules of the Music Road

- **When buying important gear for your studio, consider buying two pieces of an economically priced unit, so that you have a backup.** Yeah, I know how nice it would be to have a Focusrite compressor in your rack; but having lived to reap the benefits of being able to finish my projects because I had a couple of ART tube units on hand instead, I'd say go with the backup over the single higher-priced item.

- **Make friends with your fellow studio owners, and start thinking of them as fraternity brothers instead of competitors.** When you have a technical problem, it may be easier to fix if helped by another facility that's faced the very same problem before. In my own business, there have been many times when I have lent or borrowed equipment, or swapped tips with a fellow studio owner during an emergency.

- **Try to do as much business with your local music stores as possible.** During equipment failures, I have been able to borrow brand new items on a trial basis to get me through a tough time. Music retailers like to make their best customers happy. Mail order vendors can afford some great pricing, but local music stores can provide career-saving service and support.

- **When something does go wrong—and it will—don't panic.** Take the time to think about what is required to fix it, and how long it will be before you are operational again. Once you have this in perspective, call a meeting with your clients and tell them exactly what happened and what your game plan is. You can reschedule studio time or find another studio to help you with the work in a pinch. Clients are people too, and are generally quite forgiving and receptive to working through things if you level with them.

- **Keep your studio neat and your equipment well maintained.** Keep your studio clean and orderly so that when glitches do happen, you will be ready to deal with them head on. You can't be organizing miles of cables, cleaning up old pizza boxes and beer bottles, and searching for owner's manuals when you are trying to remedy a problem.

Learn When and Why to Say "No"

Turning business down, especially in the early stages of your career when revenue is not bountiful, is hard. Oddly enough, though, sometimes turning away a project is the best thing you can do to grow your business in the long run. Earlier I gave an example of an instance when I took on a project that I knew would really push the limits of my capabilities and creativity. In the end, that project worked out beautifully because I made a well-thought-out decision and had a realistic plan for completing the work. However, there were also times when I didn't take on projects because I decided that, for the good of the client and my own reputation, it was better to say no. You'll undoubtedly face similar situations with your business. Making the correct decision can affect your career dramatically.

You have to learn to balance the fine line between taking on projects that challenge and push you to new heights, and taking on those that will create anguish. Finding a balance between being an aggressive studio owner and a smart businessperson will take a little bit of time and some seat-of-the-pants experience. The first step in finding that balance is to take stock of your capabilities and target your efforts to find projects that fall within your comfort zone.

After I'd been in business for about a year, I gained a lot of local recognition and notoriety for my work. I did a very good job of meeting just about everybody in the local music community, and getting my accomplishments highlighted in the local newspapers and at community events. Because of my hard work, I got a lot of referrals, and my clientele grew.

At one point, I came across a tantalizing opportunity that promised to catapult my reputation forward light-years, but my better judgment prompted me to refuse the opportunity, which, as it turned out, was one of the best decisions I ever made. I was introduced to Grammy Award-winning Christian artist Kenny Eldridge at a local music store. He acknowledged my reputation and paid me several very flattering compliments, suggesting that he might like to have me mix some tunes that he had recorded out of town. I was incredibly excited that an artist of his caliber would consider gracing my humble studio with his presence.

I reveled in thinking what a coup it would be to add his name to my client roster. However, the more I thought about this project, the more I realized that I did not have the equipment necessary to properly mix a project of this level. As nice as it would have been to notch my holster with his mixes, it would have been horrible to send him away dissatisfied simply because my ego was too big. Rather than risk a fiasco, I subtly hinted to Kenny that there was a full-blown recording facility nearby with a great engineer to boot.

In the end, Kenny elected to do his mixes at the recommended studio, and I gained a great friend in its owner. For that one referral, my new friend and fellow studio owner sent me numerous projects over the years, which he was either too busy to handle or was simply not set up to service.

I have to admit also that along my learning path there were times when I elected to accept projects that I really should have walked away from for one reason or another. One such project happened in the spring of 1999. I was booked up beyond my wildest dreams when a female country singer and her husband approached me to produce a four-song demo. Unfortunately, my studio was so busy that the only hours we could possibly work together were weekends after 10 PM. The couple was willing to pay a premium rate for my services, and I had so much enthusiasm and adrenaline pumping at the time, I decided to take the project on.

Sparing all the gory details of this mess, I will say that, not only did I nearly die of sleep deprivation, but also my overextending of myself affected the quality of my work for all my other clients. On several occasions, my sessions ran too long, and I wasn't able to set up in time for scheduled appointments. I even had to cancel sessions because I was exhausted. That spring could have been a wonderful time for me. Instead, my poor decisions made it a living hell. My work suffered, and in the eyes of my clients, my reputation did, too.

By learning the limitations of your equipment and physical abilities, and by understanding the needs of your clients, you will be able to choose which projects to work on and, equally as important, which ones to avoid.

 **Walk the Walk**

One of the keys to your eventual success in this industry is the impression you make on others. I have heard very talented people in the music industry introduce themselves as *aspiring* singers, producers, or studio owners. Why the self-deprecation? If you're working in your chosen field, you're already there. Aspiring to be a better engineer or producer does not mean that you are not a legitimate engineer or producer *now*. Too often, we convince ourselves that we are not truly professionals until we have done something that attains national acclaim.

In reality, no matter how small your studio is, you are a studio owner. Just because you don't have nationally known recording artists as clients does not mean that you are not in the same profession as the big guys. The fact that one day you aspire to have a Neve console and all the trimmings has nothing to do with the fact that today you are in business, on your level, as a studio owner.

When someone asks you about your line of work, tell him or her about it. Don't be shy. Introduce yourself just as proudly as the owner of a major studio would. You've read the same magazines, perhaps belong to the same professional organizations, and strive just as they do to deliver the best-sounding recordings that your talent and equipment will allow. Those are the real qualifications of a recording studio professional.

Carry yourself as a studio owner twenty-four hours a day, and others will view and perceive you the same way. One of the ways great actors deliver believable performances is by living, eating, and sleeping the parts they play on screen long in advance of their performance. If you spend time visualizing yourself in the role of a successful studio owner, those around you will do likewise, and you will begin building a reputation as an expert in the field you love.

Get Over Yourself!

The ability to record and reproduce music is indeed a talent that is bestowed upon us. Like most studio junkies, I get excited every time I listen to a perfectly recorded snare drum or a lusciously captured acoustic guitar on one of my works; so I understand your enthusiasm. However, you should understand that as perfect as your own recordings may be, recording perfection is not enough to deliver the success you crave if your talents are unknown. No product sells itself. Plumbers, carpenters, tailors, chefs, etc., are all blessed with talents; but if the public isn't aware of them, they don't get the opportunity to practice their trades.

Over the years, I've heard countless musicians and artists scoff at the idea of having to market, sell, and otherwise sweat for their art; but to achieve success worthy of our talent and passion, we have to deal with the same indignations people in every vocation suffer. Like it or not, if you want to grow your business, it is going to take insight, and hard, smart, work, along with a willingness to realize that the road to success in the arts is the same one used by every other profession. While there is a lot of romance, passion, and mystique associated with our industry, it will be your choice to leverage all the free energy and attention your vocation can bring, or to sit on your hands waiting for business to come to you.

The bottom line is that, once you accept the fact that you have to operate your studio just like any other business, you will start to grow and reap the rewards of increased community awareness and respect—immediately. At that point, the recognition and income you seek will not be far behind. I promise.

Success Is a Process, Not an Event

Everyone has dreams, and they are all different. To be truly successful in this business, you need to think long-term and keep setting new goals; it is unlikely that one major event is going to make your career. Instead, you have to have a business plan that builds on each accomplishment and gets you focused on your future. The most successful people are those who do not sit back on their laurels, but chase new challenges and set new goals.

For instance, you might aspire to learn an 8-bus Mackie board. Having done that, you now realize that learning the famous Neve console is within your abilities, which resets your goals for that task. Or, you may aspire to have your recordings accepted by a local independent label, and after achieving that, find you have the confidence to win over the attention of major labels. The point is that there are always new horizons!

In this business, I've seen people desperately searching for that one magical contact that will put them over the edge, catapult their career to the top, and put them on Easy Street. Countless artists, producers, songwriters, and engineers have asked me questions such as, "How do I get discovered?" or "How can I get my big break?" While we've all heard stories of artists whose careers skyrocket overnight, the truth of the matter is that success generally comes as a result of hard work, coupled with a sound business plan and clear-cut goals. I'll bet that most of these so-called overnight successes would tell you that they developed their careers in a disciplined way (such as is described in this book!).

As you think about your own career path, take a look at the two examples plotted on Tables A and B. Table A (top of page 8) describes how most people view their careers: as a flat line filled with frustrations, meaningless events, and daily struggles that lead up to that "big bang" event that will make them famous. Looking at your own career in this manner is self-deprecating; it minimizes your accomplishments and creates an aura of helplessness, which will do nothing but stifle your career development. The little things you do *every single day* are what gets you where you want to go, and are the important things to focus on.

Cherish and be proud of each one of your accomplishments. Consider every project you complete to be a career building block. When you finalize your first full CD recording, be proud; don't slight yourself because it wasn't with an Aerosmith or a Mozart. Hold your head high knowing that you just trod new ground. As long as your career path keeps adding steps, no matter how small they are, you will be moving toward your long-term goals.

Do you imagine that, following a Number One hit, a new artist can simply sit back and reap the benefits of his or her success forever? Artists lose their record deals every day of the week, so they are always looking for new markets, new venues for record sales, and new execs to woo just in case they lose their current gigs. Successful people find ways to accomplish new things, however little, every day of their lives.

At the end of my own workday, for example, I make sure that I can look back on it and be proud of something—having met a new band or some new people at the musician's union or the music store, or having done *something* that will move my business forward. If you want to succeed in your business, get smart. Stop worrying about how to get to the top and focus on moving one step further along than you were when the day began. Follow a career path more along the lines of the one outlined in Table B (bottom of page 8) and your path to success will be a lot more enjoyable since you will truly be able to sit back and appreciate your own accomplishments along the way.

Table A – Perceived Career Development

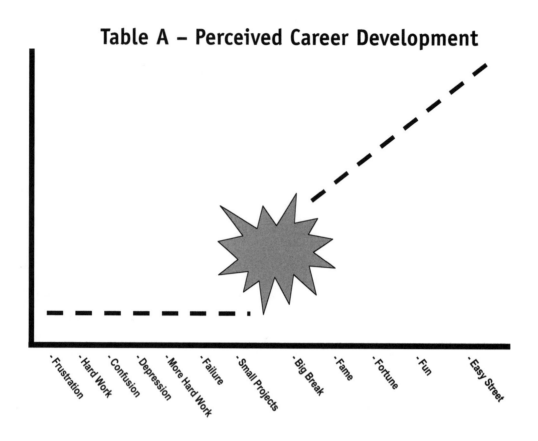

Frustration · Hard Work · Confusion · Depression · More Hard Work · Failure · Small Projects · Big Break · Fame · Fortune · Fun · Easy Street

Table B – Career Development: A Realistic Approach

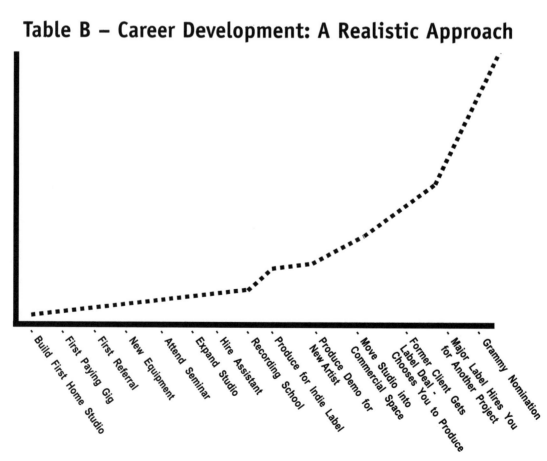

Build First Home Studio · First Paying Gig · First Referral · New Equipment · Attend Seminar · Expand Studio · Hire Assistant · Recording School · Produce for Indie Label · Produce Demo for New Artist · Move Studio into Commercial Space · Former Client Gets Label Deal, Chooses You to Produce · Major Label Hires You for Another Project · Grammy Nomination

chapter 2
Sales Techniques

Of all the material covered in this book, I suspect that no other chapter will stir an emotional response quite like this one. For some reason, people involved in the arts often feel that their work, standing alone on its own merit, should be all that is necessary to yield the commercial success and recognition they deserve. I have heard artists actually express contempt for the idea of having to sell their work. This attitude is a big obstacle to success! The truth is that if you don't sell, you don't succeed. In the real world, thriving, multi-billion dollar companies depend on hard-hitting, scientifically proven sales methods to grow their businesses. Take a lesson from the pros and lose the attitude. Learn to sell!

Salesmanship is a science, and in many ways, an art. Knowing how to sell your services will give you a decided edge over your competitors in winning new business, and will earmark you as somebody special to your clients. I hear people in daily conversation say things like, "Oh, I can talk all day; I would be a great salesperson." The fact of the matter is that salesmanship involves a lot more than simply having the gift of gab or the ability to sling BS at will!

Successful salespeople:

- Listen intently to what their clients want;
- Keep meticulous records, and are able to supply prospective clients with the latest information and product knowledge;
- Know how to build solid relationships that keep customers coming back for repeat business, and encourage clients to refer friends and family members as well;
- Turn problem clients into satisfied, happy ones;
- Know how to create value for their product(s) and command a premium price for the service(s) they render;
- Are skilled at qualifying which clients actually have the budget and commitment to record.

Accomplished salespeople spend the bulk of their time with these types of prospects. *A qualified prospect represents the highest probability of doing business.*

Selling successfully is no accident! The next time you scratch your head wondering why your local insurance salesperson (seemingly) does nothing but take new orders all day, consider this: in the formative years of building that business, he or she probably did all the fundamental selling steps required to build the foundation that supports that business today. In growing your studio, you can choose to hang your sign and wait for the phone to ring, or you can learn to sell in the marketplace with vigor, confidence, and purpose.

The sections that follow will shed a little light on the subject of selling and on how to persuade prospective clients to choose you. Learn to incorporate these principles into your daily routine, and you will be amazed at the results.

Speak the Universal Language of Images

Customers bring their hopes, dreams, and musical passions to your doorstep. They've saved their hard-earned cash, and hope for that one big break that will set their career onto the road to stardom. It's important to remember that whether they come to you for a demo or a full-blown record, your clients are bearing their souls and putting their trust in your hands.

Most artists don't care about technology and don't really understand it; so instead of bewildering them with techno-talk, use words they can translate into *familiar visual images*. Use language your clients can relate to in order to really connect and bond with them. I think of this as the "universal language." Relate to your clients in this manner, and you will find that the friendly, convenient, familiar images you have created in their minds will far outlast the memories of the mathematical formulae and techno-jargon that your competitors tried to convey in their presentations.

Entertain and tantalize your prospect by talking about how roomy and spacious your studio is, instead of wasting time talking about your shiny new AKG C12VR, your acoustically tuned booths, or your new 96-bit high-tech effects unit. Convey to your clients that they will be comfortable during their sessions, and that they should feel free to bring their own lyric sheets, for instance, or even invite visitors. Tell them about how you'll deliver some of the smoothest, most lush reverbs to make their voices sound full and powerful.

Remember to stress the little things that we take for granted, but that clients may not know. For example, while "punching in" is a staple of existence to studio owners, many artists don't understand the concept. You'll score big points with your prospect when you explain that you have the ability to go over mistakes as many times as it takes to get the take right, and that they won't have to feel pressured about goofing up their recording.

One of the best non-technical selling points of my studio was that I arranged credit accounts with about a dozen of the area's best food delivery services. During long, grueling sessions, many of my clients welcomed being able to get food delivered even though they forgot to bring cash with them that particular day. It sounds silly, but it added familiarity and comfort to my business.

When speaking about your studio, think about this: *the greatest, timeless songs are ones that paint universal images in the minds of the listeners.* When you sell your services, learn to be a great "songwriter," and find ways to bond with your customers. In your studio presentation, do everything in your power to send the prospect away with a mind full of images that convey comfort, ease of operation, a welcome atmosphere, safety, and convenience. Speak a universal language and you will experience an increase in the percent of projects that you win

B Speak in Terms of Features and Benefits

A *feature* is a characteristic, trait, attribute, aspect, or element in what you are offering (whether that thing is a service or a product). A *benefit* is the advantage or assistance those features can offer. Why is this important? Because *people do not buy features, they buy benefits!* The difference between a feature and a benefit might appear subtle to you, but understanding this difference will yield lucrative results in your business.

To illustrate, consider Salesperson #1, who tells a prospective client that the new Mercedes offers full 4-wheel independent suspension, variable power assisted rack-and-pinion steering with closed-case titanium motors, high-density magnesium wheels, and V-rated 16-inch tires, just like many of the cars on the Grand Prix circuit.

Next, consider Salesperson #2, selling the same car by pointing out that the control and comfort provided by the various high-tech features have earned this vehicle the highest safety and drivability ratings in the industry; and then, emphasis is placed on the vehicle's unmatched stability in rain and snow, and the peace of mind the car offers its owners, who can rest assured that their family couldn't be safer in any other car.

Meanwhile, back in the showroom, Salesperson #1 is explaining how moving the wheel wells outward has enabled engineers to expand the trunk space from 41 cubic feet on last year's model to 44.3 cubic feet on this year's version. Back out on the lot, Salesperson #2 says, "Check out this cool trunk! You can stick two sets of golf clubs, a baby stroller, and six grocery bags in there, and still have room left over for a briefcase and bankers box of file folders!"

Salesperson #1 is selling features, and is probably boring his prospect. Salesperson #2 is selling benefits, speaking a universal language, and creating images that the prospect can actually feel and relate to.

So how does this work in the studio? Here's an example:

Studio Owner #1 sells his services by saying, "My digital recorder allows me to put your music on a hard drive just like your computer, and I don't have to worry about storing it on tape. I can also do digital editing and punch-ins on the fly."

Studio Owner #2 sells herself this way: "By not using tape, I can rewind immediately. This allows you to spend more of your studio time actually recording, instead of waiting for the tape to roll back. This efficiency will also give you more passes at getting a part right, and more time to experiment with creative options during your sessions."

Be a Great Listener and Take Notes

If you are like me, you love your studio—the equipment, the sound, the customers—in fact, just about everything about it. That enthusiasm is infectious, and you should always include it when marketing your business. However, you need to temper that excitement when making presentations to new clients, and focus instead on *listening*. Listening makes people feel comfortable and accepted, and gives you more information to satisfy their needs.

When a prospective client comes to you for an initial consultation, do yourself a favor and resist the temptation to tell them the complete history of your marvelous studio, and all the wonderful projects you have worked on. Instead, open your mouth only to encourage your prospects to talk more about *themselves* and what *they* want. Prompted the right way, clients will tell you exactly what they are looking for in a studio, and without even realizing it, will give you the secrets to winning their business. Just listen and ask the right questions.

Take the time to ask questions about their past recording experiences. Find out what they liked and disliked. Ask them if they find anything puzzling about the recording process. Encourage them to talk about how they got started in music. Ask them about their accomplishments. Do whatever you can do to get them chatting with you. This way, you will form a bond that will make them feel a connection to you. If you really want to make prospects feel important, take notes when they says something important.

The guiding principle is this: people like to do business with people who make them feel comfortable. Take the time to listen to your customers, and they won't go anywhere else to record. Plus, details matter. It's amazingly effective, for instance, to call a prospect two weeks after meeting him or her, and to know enough about them to ask how their son's Little League game turned out. (the game you were smart enough to make a note about when the two of you spoke). That's personal involvement!

Develop and Implement the Client Profile Sheet

In addition to helping you create a relationship with your prospects and clients, a *customer profile sheet* will help you to find new sales, keep track of existing customers, and learn more about the way you do business. In fact, it's the best way to maximize and leverage the info you get from each your clients. If you use this sheet for your notes, you'll make each client feel important and confident that you are truly interested in him or her as a person—not just as a meal ticket.

Use the client profile sheet as a tool to build rapport. Explain that in order to give your clients the best service possible, you like to get to know them and input that information into your database. Put the profile on a clipboard and fill it out in front of the prospect as you converse. I've always found that clients are reassured of your sincerity and react more responsively when you take notes during the conversation.

One of the things you will learn in the selling process is that you're likely to see a client come back to you again, even if he or she have gone somewhere else to record the first time. Never assume that because a person chooses not to do business with you today that he or she won't do business with you on another project somewhere down the road. There's always another day, another project, another chance. You intend to be in the studio business for the long haul, and artists likewise intend to be recording for years to come. Logically then, *the more information you have about a prospect, the better you will be able to serve him or her the next time around.*

Whatever works for you in taking your client profile is fine, but I strongly recommend that you use the same form for every prospect you talk to, whether in person or on the phone. Use it any time you meet a potential client to document when, what, where, why and how. It might seem like unnecessary paperwork at first, but as time passes, you will have developed an excellent database of marketable prospects.

1. Maximize Your Use of the Profile:

Your file of potential clients will grow surprisingly fast. Keep track of why you won or lost a project, what type of project it was, and even what part of town it came from. This will sharpen your sales and marketing efforts and help you to grow your business even faster. Here are a few pointers that will maximize the utility of this form:

- Get to know everybody. Asking for the names and addresses of band members gives you additions to your future client lists. Bands tend to break up. If they have a producer, you might get more clients from him or her. Producers are great contacts.

- Determine what their budget is. This will help you to devise a service they can afford. Financially qualifying a prospect also prevents you from spending excessive time on those who really cannot afford your services

- Ask for an emergency contact. It's always a good idea when somebody is working at your facility.

- Summarize critical notes after the client leaves. Keep track of your pricing, the points that you felt won or lost the project, and any comments the client may make about your studio.

- Know where the artists perform. This will give you new places to go to meet new bands, and give you insight into the sound they relate to.

The following is a sample of a typical customer profile sheet:

NAME_____   DATE_____

ADDRESS _____   PHONE_____

_____   E-MAIL _____ _____

_____

STYLE _____

PROJECT TYPE _____

START DATE_____   FINISH DATE _____

BUDGET_____   PRODUCER_____

BAND MEMBERS _____

_____

_____

EMERGENCY PHONE _____

HOW DID YOU FIND OUT ABOUT US?_____

WHERE DO YOU CURRENTLY
PERFORM?_____

_____   _____

STUDIO
NOTES_____

_____

_____

_____

_____

_____

Proposals and Follow-Ups

1. Proposals

Maintaining a good account of your business events and transactions goes hand-in-hand with keeping accurate customer profile information. It's very easy for a private studio owner to do business on a verbal or handshake basis, but it's a serious mistake. Nobody likes mindless paperwork, but I've learned over time that the downside of not having documentation of conversations, services promised, pricing, and project specifics is far more troublesome than actually doing the paperwork.

As your business grows, the number of people that you have quoted pricing to will grow faster than you can ever imagine. Keeping track of what you said to whom will become a daunting task. I strongly urge you to develop the habit of recording everything you discuss with a customer in writing.

For example, if a guy walks in off the street and wants to buy four hours of time to record his kid playing the kazoo, take the time to write out a little proposal and have him sign it. Eighteen months down the line, when he tries to tell you that you did the work for $35.00/ hour and gave him five CDs, you can show him that he paid $45.00/hour and bought the CDs separately. With these projects, nothing is worse than quoting a new project at $65.00/hour, only to have your head chewed off because the client still had his receipt from eighteen months ago showing that you charged him $45.00/hour. Documentation will make your life a lot easier.

For smaller projects, use your computer to print out a quick, standard contract with just a few essential details. For larger projects, invest the time to put together a custom offering using the information gained in the interview and recorded on the profile sheet.

As you work on projects, no matter how perfect the client seems, you are going to run into problems, misunderstandings, and disagreements. Nothing makes solving these problems easier than pulling out a neatly typed proposal that proudly displays the signatures of both you and your client. "See Bob, right there on line 6 it says that the client shall supply the engineer with all the beer he can drink." No mix-ups! No misunderstandings! No disagreements!

Having a proposal document will not only help you keep disagreements to a minimum, but it also will give you a historical record of your pricing strategies and your ability to finish projects on time. In addition, proposals are one of the most effective sales techniques that you can apply. Make a practice of pitching for the project in every proposal you send out. Each one of my proposals ends with a phrase similar to this one: "I appreciate the opportunity to offer my services and hope that I may be favored with your business." Always ask for the business. This is a principle of every single kind of selling situation, not just the recording business. Put your own spin on it, but do it—and remember to say, "Please!"

2. Follow-Ups

In addition to proposals, follow-up letters or calls, which update your clients on the progress of their projects, are essential. They're the perfect reminder to keep clients on schedule and on goal. Use follow-ups to remind clients to have the guitar player at the studio at a certain time, or to bring everyone up to date on budgets and billing. A follow-up letter is the perfect place to reiterate a change in payment arrangements or the actual pricing on a project. I use follow-up letters even when the smallest detail of the project has changed. Verbal agreements in the studio are easy to forget weeks later when the next session is scheduled.

The initial follow-up letter can be a great enticement to moving a prospect off dead center and onto booking his or her project with you. Need a reason to write?

- Inform him or her about a new piece of equipment that you obtained.
- Tell him or her about a discount that he or she is eligible for.
- Tell him or her about your referral discount deals (come up with something smart—your best sources of new customers are your existing ones!).

On a side note, if you are going to take the time to send a proposal, letter, or invoice, invest the time, money, and ingenuity on some professional-looking letterhead. Small things mean a lot when prospective clients are sizing you up. Check out the stationary section in Chapter 6, "Your Business Toolbox."

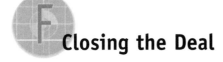 **Closing the Deal**

The easiest way to get someone to buy your product or service is also the toughest technique to learn. Asking for an order—closing the deal—is essential, no matter how you do it. While there are volumes upon volumes of books written on successful selling techniques, the undisputed champion of techniques for winning business is the simplest: *ask for it*.

Yes, it's a little uncomfortable looking your client in the eye and asking him or her, "Will you do business with me?" However, research shows that the most successful salespeople are the ones who ask for what they want. Good salespeople know that it is much easier for a prospect to say yes than it is for them to say no. Keep that in mind every time you're chasing business, and I promise that you will get more comfortable and feel more at home asking for the order—and you will definitely book more projects. To get started, I'll give you some examples of some of the more common, effective closes to use in your day-to-day operations. Each has the same objective: get the deal, or find out exactly what the prospect needs in order for you to close the deal.

1. The Direct Close

This is the most effective and simplest, yet it takes the most self-confidence to perform: simply, in a straightforward manner, ask for what you want. Examples of this close are, "Will you buy my product?" "Can I go ahead and write this order up?" "Are you ready to get started?"

2. The Assumptive Close

With this technique, you speak to the prospect as if he or she has already decided to go along with your proposal, even though he or she hasn't yet really committed to the deal. The philosophy is that people don't like to say no. By experiencing the ball rolling, many prospects will just bite their lip, skip the comparison-shopping, and go along for the ride, figuring that they must have given you the go-ahead signal. Examples of this close would be: "Okay Bob, do you want to start on the seventh or the thirteenth of this month?" Alternatively, "Mike, should I put you down for the $3,000 program or the $4,500 program?" Or, "Are you writing a check or using a credit card for the down payment?"

If the prospect does muster up the gumption to say, "No," then your assumption looks like an innocent misunderstanding, which still gives you the opportunity to continue with a different close. When he or she stops the assumptive close with a question or objection, simply ask what the concerns are, and keep drawing out his or her comments until he or she finally tells you what you need to do to win the project.

3. The List Close

I call this the "gotcha" close because it uses the prospect's own words to close him or her. A completed prospect profile form will provide you with the perfect guide to carry out the technique. You must jot down very clearly each detail of the project that your client tells you is important. Then at the end of your presentation, if your prospect replies to your initial closing attempt with either a "no," or a hesitating, "I'll have to think about it," you can take another shot at getting his or her business right then and there by reiterating the concerns stated and how you've addressed them. The dialogue would go something like this:

You: "Bob, you told me that you wanted to record in a clean, smoke-free environment. Wouldn't you agree that my place is comfortable, clean, and smoke free?"

Bob: "Well, yes, I would."

You: "Okay. And you also told me that you wanted to record on hard disk so you could save time not having to rewind tape. So my digital format will give you that feature, right?"

Bob: "Oh, yeah, it sure will."

You: "You stressed to me the importance of being able to work late hours on weekends, which I made provisions for. So recording with me would fit right into your schedule, would it not?"

Bob: "Yes, that would work out well."

You: "One of the other things you require is to be able to finish the project for about $3,000. I offered you a discount and a fixed package price that would fit that budget. So recording with me is indeed affordable to you, right?"

Bob: "Yes."

You: "Well, Bob, when you came in today, I asked you to tell me all the things you needed to make you happy in completing this project. I really believe I have offered you all those benefits; so can you tell me what else I need to offer you to win your project? Is there something you asked for that I am not delivering?"

At this point, Bob may or may not award you the job, but your chances are better than they would have been if you simply had let Bob walk out the door, claiming he needed time to think about it.

4. The Follow-Up Close

If Bob will still not commit right then and there, make sure you have noted his concerns before he leaves. Ask his permission to follow up with him on the telephone in a few days. Once Bob agrees, take out your appointment book to record a specific appointment for a day and time to speak on the phone. Suggest that he mark it down, too.

You can "soft sell" the need to do this by stressing that his project is important to you; and since you're both busy, a firm appointment time makes sense. If Bob doesn't have an appointment book with him, write out an appointment reminder card for him. Trust me; if you make an appointment to call him at Friday at 3 PM, chances are he will be there to answer the phone. If not, when you do get in touch with him again, he's likely to give you his undivided attention because of your attention to detail.

In essence, no close can make a person do business with you when they don't want to. However, more often than not, a good closing technique can turn a "no" into a "yes." In an ideal world, your charming personality, reputation for excellence, and studio savvy will have the client committing to doing business with you—without your ever having to ask for it. That's when business is really fun! Just in case things don't happen that easily, remember to go for the close at the end of your presentation. If the prospect doesn't commit to you, he or she is still a viable future business opportunity; so it's up to you to harvest that opportunity by trying to close him or her. If you don't, somebody else will.

5. The Expiration Dating, or X-Dating, Close

This little gem comes from my old Metropolitan Insurance agent. Back in the formative years of my selling career, I spent a few hours listening to my agent's telephone style in an effort to improve upon my own sales success. Technically, expiration dating, or X-dating for short, is not a closing technique, but a clever way of getting a future communication date with your prospect. It can lead you to more sales opportunities, and afford you an effective way to keep an open line of communication going with even the most difficult prospects.

Here is the way Ernie Schmidlap, my insurance agent, utilized X-dating:

Ernie: "I would like to give you a competitive price on your automobile insurance."

Prospect: "Well, Ernie, I have insurance with one of your competitors."

Ernie: "Oh, I see, very well. So how long is that paid up for?"

Prospect: It's not due until August 30th of next year."

Ernie: Okay, well then, I really don't want to consume your time now, but how about if I call you back on August 1st, before you renew, to see if I can't give you better service and save you some money?"

Prospect: (Glad to be able to get off the phone, but at least open to saving some money). "Ah, yeah, sure that will be good."

Essentially, Ernie gave himself a reason to talk to his prospect again, thereby increasing his chances of making the sale. Simple but effective! In the above example, X-dating used the prospect's insurance expiration date as a starting point for building a client relationship. I have modified this technique to work very nicely for increasing my opportunities for winning new recording clients. Here are a just a few examples of how it can work for you:

Example 1

Client: "Well, I looked at your proposal and it looks good, but I just don't have the funds right now."

You: "I can understand that—I have a lot of bills myself. So let me ask this: 'Do you want to record your project with me eventually?' If so, I can extend the effective date of the proposal, and call you in two months to see how your finances are. Would that be helpful?"

Example 2

Client: "Oh, I would love to record with you, but we are not quite ready yet because our new guitar player is still learning his parts."

You: "Makes sense. How about if I call you in four weeks to see how things are coming along? That way, as you progress, I can keep you apprised of my studio schedule so that you can book the time when you are finally ready."

Other potential obstacles to overcome:

- "We are not ready to record our next project yet."
- "We haven't really settled on our song selections yet."
- "Our keyboard player quit and we need to find a new one."
- "Hey man, my girlfriend and I are fighting right now…"

When faced with these kinds of objections, first inquire as to what their proposed solutions might be, and offer some help where you can. Then choose a reasonable time limit to solve the problem. Determine an X-date, then make an appointment to follow-up. In many instances, simply being there to listen and help prospects work through their difficulties may be enough to win such projects. These types of situations are excellent opportunities to distinguish yourself as someone who cares about his or her clients.

chapter 3
Marketing Techniques

If good selling techniques are the K.O. punch of your business, then marketing is your jab to set it all up. In its complete scope, marketing includes many different facets:

- Price determination
- Discounting strategy
- Target marketing
- Advertising strategy
- Trade promotions
- Other tactics and strategies that help promote your business

It is important to a get a clear, concise, simple definition of marketing within the context of this book so that we can go about the business of getting you more business. The most effective and easy-to-understand definition that I have ever seen is this:

Marketing is the action of letting others know about you.

This definition is pure, straightforward, and makes thinking about your marketing efforts easy. As you go through the trials and tribulations of running your business, I want you to print this message out in bold typeface, and then display it openly in a prominent place so that you can't avoid seeing it on a daily basis. In those times when business is slow, I want you to look at this definition and ask yourself, "What have I done to market my business *today*?" In those times when business is jamming along famously, I *still* want you to look at the definition, and ask yourself the same question!

Another important point:

The more people who know about your business, the more likely you are to succeed.

This is the reason big companies like Microsoft use every imaginable method to let you know who they are. They use TV, radio, print, mailers, sporting event banners, and department store promotions to tell people who they are and what they do.

For a small, independent business, developing a marketing plan may seem like a monumental task, as well as a financial strain. You only have so much time and money to spend, right? Good news! A limited budget and a one-person staff shouldn't prevent you from marketing yourself successfully. Just keep in mind that, for right now, your marketing campaign does not have to rival that of the multimillion-dollar corporations; in fact, it doesn't even have to rival that of your local competitors. The only real requirement of your personal marketing campaign should be that it successfully introduces your business to new audiences—hopefully those with a concentration of potential clients! While some schemes don't have enough potential to warrant a great deal of your resources, there is nearly always business to be uncovered in places you might never have thought to look.

There is potential business everywhere. Be on the lookout for new opportunities, and you will be surprised at the places you find them:

- That little old lady in line in front of you in the grocery store just may have a granddaughter who is looking for a producer.
- The guy that sold you a car today may know a polka band looking to record a CD to sell at their shows.
- Your neighbor might work at the factory with an aspiring solo pianist who would like to record herself (but never knew there was a studio in town).

You absolutely must exploit the most marvelous and effective marketing tool that you will ever have—your ability to talk about your business. Talk, talk, talk, talk it up, no matter where you are—at the car wash; doctor's office; church; on trains, buses, planes, etc.

Make sure that you tell people what you do as often as possible. (If you really want to be wild, you can turn the tables on those annoying telemarketers that call at dinnertime. Stop them dead in their tracks and talk about what *you* want to sell to *them!*) Your business is exciting, and people will love to hear about it. When they do, they'll tell their friends.

Over the years, I have found numerous techniques to get people to converse with me about the music business; and with a little practice, you can develop useful techniques, too. For instance, if a guy tells you he hates his job, tell him that you love yours. I guarantee he'll ask you what you do for a living; and when you tell him, he (or maybe even the person standing next to the two of you, eavesdropping) is going to know someone who is a musician or artist, and show some interest.

No, you don't want to turn into a cold and calculating robot programmed to talk about music no matter what the topic of conversation is, but it is good to realize that talking about what you do for a living is ear candy to most of those poor slobs who punch a time clock to earn a living.

SALES TIP! *The group of sixth graders who parade through your studio on a field trip may leave some gum stuck under your console, but they will also provide you with more word-of-mouth advertising than you could ever hope for. Show and tell, baby; show and tell!*

Business Cards

In conjunction with your newfound fluency in talking with others about your business, a well-designed business card is an absolute necessity for developing a successful marketing campaign. Nothing makes a conversation memorable like a business card. Earlier on in this book, I talked about "walking the walk," and how, if you present yourself as a successful business owner, the community will perceive you that way. It doesn't matter whether your studio consists only of a 4-track cassette unit in your bedroom, or a 128-channel Neve-based monster located on a pastoral estate; having a business card that makes an impressive statement about your studio is an absolute must.

If you are on a limited budget, today's computer-printing technology will make acquiring attractive, effective business cards a relatively simple matter. Any office supply retailer can have them to you in as little as two days! I prefer having professionally printed cards because they generally offer more options in terms of card stock, ink, and graphics; but you can even print them out on your personal computer if your budget is tight (remembering to use the heaviest card stock you can find and to print them on a laser printer). Whichever method you choose, it is important that the card be clear, concise, and able to get your point across.

A card that that says too little can be a detriment to your efforts, and a card that says too much could hit the wastebasket. When designing a card, try to remember that people are busy and therefore often have short attention spans. Think about your own life! Do you always have enough time for the things you want to do? Do your days always go as planned? Of course not! So when you're designing your card, remember that your potential customers live in the same crazy, hectic world that you do. They will appreciate a card that is clear and easy to read.

You'll likely be handing your card to someone after the two of you have had some initial conversation about your business, so don't be redundant with information. Resist the temptation to list every one of your products and services on your card. You'll never find enough space on a business card to list *everything*, and you don't want a card that causes confusion. Be cognizant of the fact that the more stuff you list, the smaller the font will have to be—and smaller fonts are a challenge to read. You've probably built your studio to offer convenience to your clients; design your business card to offer the same.

The critical elements of a good business card are:

- Your company's name
- Your basic service (if that's not clear from the name of your business)
- Your name
- Your phone number
- Your email address
- Your website address

Each item needs to be of a substantial font size and easily readable, no matter where on the card it's placed. Don't make it difficult for people to find the information that their already overtaxed brains are seeking.

Devote no more than one line to your services and popular offerings, and keep it simple. Mentioning your wonderful equipment might make you feel proud, but it will do nothing but clutter up your card and diminish its overall message. If the name of your business is "Digital Recording Studios," you don't need to reiterate the fact that you offer digital recording. If your prospects want further specifics, they can always contact you.

Unless you have a receptionist to handle customers who just come in from off the street, I urge you not to list your entire business address on the card. There is nothing worse than having an important session interrupted by a couple of teens who decided it would be cool to drop by and see what your place looks like. I suggest that you run your studio business by appointment only. When a genuine prospect calls or emails, you will have the opportunity to give him or her directions to your little slice of heaven.

An email address and/or website is important because those people who are seeking basic information, or who are not quite ready to commit to you, are apt to drop you a line versus giving you a call. Acquiring a prospect's email address is like winning the lottery because it costs you nothing to market to them! (More on this later.)

The most effective business cards are those that use a substantial and tasteful card stock. Bright white, eggshell, light gray, or light blue are all good color choices. Avoid card stock in unusual colors like black, bright orange, or shiny gold, which can be perceived as unsightly and unprofessional, make the typeface difficult to read, and may say things about you to some people that you didn't intend to say!

Keep your ink selections down to no more than two colors for maximum readability. Textured stock can add a professional flair to your card, and its visual energy is memorable. A cleverly designed music theme logo integrated into your card (and your other marketing materials) is a nice touch, and will make it stand out.

The following are four examples of very different business card designs (on which I've substituted my own information; only 2 and 4 are actually my cards) to illustrate these points. Three of the cards I consider to be well designed; one I feel to be poorly designed.

TUNEMAN PRODUCTIONS

TOM VOLINCHAK
OWNER

101 Riverview Drive, Suite 101 • Memphis, TN 38103
(901) 579-9327 • Fax: (901) 579-9999 • Cell: (901) 579-0000
Email:TomVolinchak@aol.com • Website: www.tunemanproductions.com

I absolutely love this card! The "golden egg" theme conveys a strong visual image of wealth, prosperity, and security. Simple, but effective.

Tom Volinchak
Licensing Executive
General Licensing

10 Music Square East, Nashville, TN 37203-4399
(800) 925-8451 ext. 2855 Fax: (615) 401-2829
E-Mail: tvolinchak@bmi.com

This BMI card leaves absolutely no doubt as to where the card originated or the business it represents. All the important details are likewise easy to find. This is a perfect example of an easy-to-read card.

Tuneman Productions
101 Riverview Drive, Suite 101
Memphis, TN 38103
Website: www.tunemanproductions.com

Tom Volinchak
Owner

phone: (901) 579-9327
~~cell: (901) 579-9999~~
~~www.tunemanproductions.com~~

Tom Volinchak @ aol. com

901 579 0000

This card is confusing enough to test the patience of Job! In addition to its hard-to-read, jumbled-up text, which is crammed into the topmost section of the card, the barely legible, hand-scribbled email address and revised phone number make this card a nightmare.

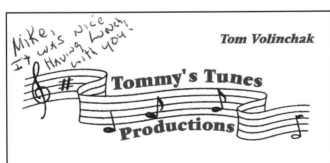

Mike, It was nice having lunch with you!

Tom Volinchak

Tommy's Tunes
Productions

Recording • CD's • Cassettes   Phone: (901) 579-9327
Radio Promotion • Commercials   E-mail: tommytuneman@aol.com

This card is the most indicative of personal style. Its incorporation of a music-oriented graphic make it truly representative of the industry in which I do my business, and the business name connotes the type of business it is—as well as whose business it is!

SALES TIP! *One of my first sales mentors taught me a little business card trick, which has had great results. When you hand your business card to someone, no matter where you are, take the time to jot a personal note on the front (see Business Card 4, page 25). It doesn't have to be elaborate, just enough to call attention to your card. Something simple like, "Ralph, it was great having lunch with you," or, "Sally, thanks for sharing your music with me," is fine. Research has shown that a person is much more likely to keep a business card that has a personal message written on the front. A message personalizes an otherwise non-personal communication, and provides its recipient with a sort of visual remembrance of your encounter.*

You'll be amazed at the business that will come your way with this simple technique. I landed one of my largest clients ever, a church, through a business card that I casually handed to someone else three years before, which bore a small message I'd jotted down on the front. Seeing it again when the client visited my studio hammered home just how effective this technique is. I instantly recalled not only the person I originally gave it to, but also the events surrounding that meeting.

B Memorable Graphics

Mega-companies such as Nike, Pepsi, and Anheuser-Busch have been reaping huge benefits for years, due in large part to their clever, catchy visual images.

Take a pointer or two from these success stories and incorporate some graphic wizardry into your own marketing efforts. People remember images and sounds more vividly than they do text; and believe it or not, you don't have to pay an expensive design firm to come up with catchy visuals.

For example, if your name is Mark Green, you could use green ink on your business cards, call your business "Studio Green," and use green CDs for your demo. At one of my recent seminars, we were talking about new ideas that would help someone's business be memorable. One attendee told us that his last name was Speckle. You can imagine the cool ideas that flowed. If it were my business, *everything* would be speckled!

The use of visual images shouldn't be limited to your stationary and other business products and promotional aids; you can become a virtual, walking billboard for your business by being memorable in person. Here is an example: when I first moved to Nashville, I only knew a few people and had to grow my business to sustain me. There were so many studios and producers in Nashville. I felt like a needle in a haystack, convinced that I would never be noticed.

One day, at my favorite Music Row restaurant, the owner (who had noticed that I frequently wore a pair of bright red, patent-leather air walkers) shouted to me, "Hey, Red Shoes, how the hell ya doin?" At that moment my publishing company, Hot Red Shoes-BMI was born, and I started wearing red shoes everywhere in public. Wacky? Sure, but it was a lot easier for people to remember Tommy Red Shoes than it was to remember Tommy Volinchak. In my first month in Nashville, my reputation for wearing red shoes brought me more attention and recognition than any amount of radio, TV, or print advertising could have.

Next, I started a record label called "Red Shoe Records." I even put a pair of outrageous, 5-inch-heeled, women's red pumps on top of my near field monitors. Talk about being noticed! I found a jpeg of a similar pair and added it to all my publishing and recording contracts. When I conducted music business, I always wore red shoes (as did my assistants).

Red shoes aren't for everybody, but you might find that a theme or gimmick will add panache to your presentation, and differentiate your marketing efforts from your competitors. Nicknames, habits, pets, automobiles, and even the foods you like to eat might be sources for your marketing identity. Generally, the simplest things turn out to be the most memorable.

Promotion

1. When Buying Advertising, Beware!

The very first dime you spend on advertising should probably be on a Yellow Pages ad. Look at your local book and check out the competition's ads. Other studios' presence in the listings should tell you a lot about what type and size of ad you need to get noticed by anyone looking for a studio. Chances are good that an effective ad in the Yellow Pages will bring you enough cold business to make it a worthwhile investment—especially if you are just starting out and looking for new business.

TV, radio, and print advertising offer wonderful results when used the right way—but they're costly. To be truly effective, media advertising must be highly visible and presented to the public consistently. Prime-time and front-page advertising may be out of the price range of most individual studio owners. But fortunately, you don't need to compete in this megabucks arena to find effective advertising for yourself. Other solutions exist. Buying advertising can feel like walking through a minefield, so be prepared to ask a lot of questions and:

- **Know *what* you are buying.** Find out when and how it will appear, and for what length of time.

- **Know *who* is likely to see it.** Find out, in terms of total number and by age groups, what sector of the population will see it.

- **Know *when* and *how often* the ad will appear.** If it's a broadcast ad, what percentage of the viewing audience will be exposed to airtime?

- **Know the cost structure.** It's always negotiable, especially if you buy space in more than one issue of a printed publication, or more than just a couple of air dates on radio or TV.

- **Know what your competitors are running.** If anything, and where and when their ads appear.

Most advertising salespeople starve if they don't sell, but they don't usually have a problem finding well-funded companies to suck up the prime ad space on the highest-rated TV shows, most visible commercial space, or the front page of the newspaper section applicable to the ad's particular business. Where ad salespeople differentiate themselves from their competition is in the selling of *secondary space.*

I call this space the "Forbidden Fruit of the Garden of Ad-en." These silver-tongued, snake-oil-vendor-like salespeople will offer ad space that sounds like the deal of a lifetime. But after you take a bite out of this fruit, you will feel naked. Trust me! When I first went into the studio business, I was enthusiastic and prepared to shoot the works on advertising. Since no other local studio advertised on the radio (or so I thought), I was convinced that this was the road to instant riches. A quick conversation with my local radio ad salesperson, "Herman St. Lucifer," confirmed my beliefs.

Ol' Herman was even more excited about my idea to do a radio campaign than I was. Hell's fire! I was on to something! Herman sold me four weeks of economical radio space consisting of twenty 20-second spots on what he called "second tier positions." He assured me that while these were not prime-time spots, at the discounted rates they still delivered 90% of the audience that the prime-time spots did (clearly, in retrospect, a bold-faced lie!). He further tantalized me with the added benefit of assuring me that the DJs would probably pop my ad into some prime-time spots when their programming didn't begin or end exactly on schedule. (If you get this spiel, don't believe it. If someone promises bonus units, get in writing exactly what the bonus spots consist of, at what times they will run, and the duration of time over which—days, weeks, months—they will air.

I quickly found out that during a 168-hour week, my twenty ads amounted to one impressive 20-second blurb every 8.4 hours. You think that sounds bad? Think about it this way: for every 30,240 seconds of radio airtime, my ads took up twenty seconds—one second for every 1,512 seconds of airtime. Talk about a needle in a haystack! To make matters worse, the ad was being played at the most ridiculous hours of the day and during programs nobody was listening to. This was a $1,000 lesson that I would prefer you learn here.

Here's an exercise that will help you get a real feel for just how frequently a radio campaign should air to be effective. The next time you hear a familiar ad for a product on the radio, jot down the time it aired, and then ask a few of your friends to listen to that radio station at different times during the day. Have them keep count of how many times during an hour-long segment that the ad is repeated. Then have them share their results with you. The amount of repetition some of these ads contract for will make your head spin.

I am not saying that radio advertising will not help you grow your business—because it will. I am just pointing out that a successful media campaign will require a high rate of recurrence on the right station, within the right programming, and over a substantial period of time to be successful. Don't be fooled into thinking that a few ads on TV or radio will catapult you into immediate financial success. The same holds true for print advertising.

SALES TIP! *In the event that you do opt for some form of media advertising, here is a sure-fire method of determining if your choice is effective. If you choose print advertising, offer a discount coupon in the ad. That way someone that comes to you in response to the ad will bring the coupon along, signaling that your ad campaign successfully reached at least that individual. Likewise, if you choose radio or TV advertising, offer a special program or discount "just for mentioning the ad." Everyone loves something for nothing, and this might also be a good way to encourage people to tell their friends about your business. Of course, neither method will tell you about the people who saw or heard your ad, and only noted it for future reference.*

2. Try Something New

Some recordists believe that the highly specific nature of their service dictates that the only opportunities to effectively market and advertise for them are in places and publications that regularly cater to musicians and artists. Nothing could be further from the truth. As you proceed in your own career, you will find prospects in places and situations that you would never imagine to be breeding grounds for new business.

For example, a few years back, a friend of mine was struggling with her business, and beating her head against the wall as she tried to find effective and affordable ways to market her business of assisting attorneys with medical/legal issues. She had been spending a fortune at trade shows, on print and radio advertising, and on mailers without really turning up any new clients. We decided to have dinner and take in a movie to get her mind off of things. There it hit me: *advertise at the movies prior to the previews!*

She thought I was a little crazy, since she dealt with highly respected professionals (doctors, lawyers, administrators, etc.). She initially objected, arguing that advertising in such a way might be interpreted by her sophisticated clientele as crude. I disagreed. Don't doctors and lawyers see movies? Don't doctors and lawyers read those big-screen slide shows just as everyone else does? Ultimately, the success or failure of such a campaign depended on how many professionals would see her ad; so a test was in order.

As it turned out, the movie theaters were eager to cut a sweet deal for a new customer, and my friend was able to get her ad on a bunch of movie screens, and could therefore test the medium for peanuts. These ads consequently brought her a lot of business! Sometimes trying a very new idea is the only way to get your promotion moving (as long as it does not break your bank or jeopardize the business).

3. Bartering

Bartering is an excellent way for you to afford advertising if you can offer products and services (i.e., bumper music for local DJs and TV shows) in trade for an advertising allowance. In other words, you could offer broadcasters commercial recording in return for airtime. TV and radio stations are always looking for bargains, and I've found that local stations are usually willing to barter for the things they need (these businesses also need recorded messages for their own use, as well as for their advertisers, and often contract local production houses and studios for this purpose). The great thing about bartering for advertising is that you can negotiate an even better deal for yourself—if you stand your ground. Remember, their ad space has much less value to them when they are getting a service without a cash outlay, so be sure to emphasize the value of your services in order to get the highest rate of trade.

3. Karaoke DJs

These guys are an excellent source of advertising and business. Frequently, karaoke DJs need help hooking up and maintaining their equipment, or they may need recordings for some of their patrons and followers—services you can provide. A little work for these enterprises, in return for them placing your flyer in their songbooks, is one of the best advertising values you're likely to find.

SALES TIP! *I like to garner free advertising and increase public awareness of my business by offering recording time as a prize for local karaoke contests. Recently, I judged such a contest, and offered a 4-hour first prize, a two-hour second prize, and a one-hour third prize. The karaoke company was so thrilled that they included me in their radio advertising! For judging five nights of talent, I received five weeks of about sixteen radio spots per day. This is essentially like being fed and watered for free! I also made a ton of music contacts in the process. The radio ads brought me new business, and I met three very good vocalists and two bands, who all wanted to do a demo.*

Shameless Self-Promotion: Free Press / PR

1. Free Press / PR

Print publications have deadlines to meet and pages to fill—and are often short on reporters and good local stories. This presents you with a wonderful opportunity to get some free press. Remember, many people find the music business magical and exciting, which may make getting into your local paper a bit easier for you than the average business owner. If a newspaper announces that there is a new tire store in town, it may not grab much reader attention; but the announcement of a new recording studio in the area may.

Over the years, I have gotten a lot of free newspaper and broadcast promotion simply by presenting my business as a news story. "Local Recording Studio Develops Hometown Talent," is a storyline that garnered free local coverage. Another potential story: "Area Woman Turns Recording Hobby into a Full-Time Business." Don't overlook any media. Local trader/merchant publications and township papers are always on the lookout for stories.

2. Be a Good Citizen; Support the Arts

Be a good citizen and support your local arts by assisting local playhouses, schools, and theatre productions. You could run live sound, produce a few commercials for their shows, or even help them set up their own sound systems. In return for your services, you can usually get your studio advertised in their programs and flyers.

Consider giving a public education seminar on the music industry. Local business and community organizations are often on the lookout for people to give short, informative seminars on suitable subjects. Chances are excellent that they would be extremely receptive to a presentation about simple, inexpensive recording products and technology.

3. Music Store Bulletin Boards

A flyer or homemade tri-fold brochure is the perfect promotional tool to alert local bands and singers that you are in the marketplace. Since the traffic on these boards can be active, check your posting weekly—move it around, change the color/appearance, even make sure it's still there—in order to maximize the effectiveness of this promotional resource.

While you're at it, you can use the bulletin board to add to your potential client list. Names from a music store bulletin board are valuable for two reasons:

- Musicians talk to other musicians, and their conversations can spread the word about your studio like wildfire. If the person reading your ad has no use for recordings, he might know someone who does.
- It's a great way to reach out to players as potential hires for your projects.

Other potential opportunities for free PR are county fairs, political events, local benefit shows, and even church events. Don't forget to circulate and mingle in the clubs featuring live bands, karaoke patrons, and comedians. This is a great way to expand your clientele while having Uncle Sam pay for your weekend entertainment (because it's business-related, such expenses are tax write-offs). Also while you're out there, take the time to talk to the cats running live sound—they can be a great source of business for you. Lastly, throw yourself a "Grand Opening" party and invite everyone you know—and tell them to bring their friends. For the price of some soft drinks and chips you'll get invaluable PR!

chapter **4**
Your Business Toolbox

The Essentials You Must Have

Many recording studios extend only verbal agreements, and then wait for the client to show up. Not surprisingly, the result is that many smaller studios are struggling to keep their doors open. Let's look at some better business practices that you can employ to prosper in a competitive marketplace.

A Paperwork and Systems

Appearances are more important than you may think. It's essential to have personalized letterhead, business cards, invoices, tracking sheets, fax cover pages, and the other stationery items needed to carry on regular business interaction. If you don't, you're shooting yourself in the foot—and it's time to upgrade your mode of operation in order to expand your business.

Find a professional printer to make your stationery, or visit your local office supply retailer for help with customized printing. Unfortunately, you may not be taken as seriously with self-produced stationary (the type you print on a home computer). Great stationery is essential to your success; it will make conducting your business easier, and it will give you the look of professionalism that sets you apart from the competition.

1. Proposals

As your business grows, it may impossible for you to keep track of what prices you quoted to whom. Who would remember details quoted on the phone weeks ago—unless you have a system? Standardized proposals are essential.

A written proposal provides you with some important benefits:

- It gives you a physical record of your presentation.
- It is likely to elicit a subsequent meeting with the prospect, thereby giving you a better chance to build a relationship.
- It provides you with a face-to-face, point-by-point selling tool that competitors who only offer a verbal price lack.

Your proposal should detail such things as all the features that your session will offer, with a particular focus on any value-added services. It's also important to include an expiration date.

Ask for the business at the end of every proposal, or in the very last sentence. This lets your prospect know that their business is important to you. This is a standard practice among all successful sales professionals, and its inclusion can increase your rate of selling success. Here are some examples of good proposal closings:

- "I enjoyed your visit to my studio, and I am looking forward to recording your project."
- "I was impressed with your playing ability and hope that I may be favored with your business." (If you want your proposal to be maximally effective, ask for the order!)

a. Keep Track of Clients and Their Needs

- **Face-to-Face Proposals:** I recommend that you *never* quote a price over the phone. Instead, meet personally with each prospect, and fill out the customer profile sheet (see chapter 2) by jotting down all the information shared about the upcoming recording. At the end of that conversation, review the information with the client in order to offer him or her the best package possible, and give him or her an estimated date when you will have the proposal ready. When it's prepared, either mail the proposal and call to set up a time to follow up, or invite the client to visit your studio to go over the details together.

- **Tracking Numbers:** It is a lifesaving practice to assign a tracking number to each proposal so that you can catalog, reference, and tie it to the potential contract and invoice. This will help you correlate information regarding all future contract-related documents. As your business grows, you will develop repeat business, and many of your customers will require several revised proposals before signing on the dotted line. Ten proposals for one customer will be too confusing unless you have a manageable way to keep them organized, and in date order. Tracking numbers will take the confusion out of the proposal process.

- **Customer Numbers:** Also assigning a numeric code, or *customer number*, for each client will help you easily track pricing for that client over time and through multiple jobs. For recordkeeping purposes, remember that each tracking number should have a cross-reference to the customer number, each individual job, and date. This system will also readily tell you how many proposals you have on file for a particular customer number.

  Before completing any new proposal, you should check that customer's number to see if any other proposals are "open" (unaccepted), in process, or "closed" (completed). As your business grows, this system is essential in providing maximum customer service, price control, project tracking, and business tax return preparation.

To illustrate the proposal process, consider the following: Your new client, Melody Sweetnote, is assigned customer number 701. Her first proposal, issued in October, 2002, is number 01. This proposal tracking number then becomes **701-1002-01**. If this proposal is accepted and the project completed, you will add a fourth segment, indicating that it is a closed, or finished, job. Therefore, this tracking number consists of:

- **Customer Number: 701**. Melody's customer number. Tip: if you really want to utilize your database to its full potential, in order track where your business is coming from, assign customer numbers by categories, (i.e., 500s, karaoke; 700s, barter; 900s, rap; etc.)
- **Date: 1002.** October 2002, the date of this proposal
- **Proposal Number: 01.** This particular proposal number
- **Project Number: 05.** Added when Melody accepts the proposal and completes the project. This proposal number should then be linked to the contract, invoice, payment vouchers, etc. for cross-referencing purposes.

The following is an example of a typical proposal:

Tuneman Productions
101 Riverview Drive, Suite 101
Memphis, TN 38103
(901) 579-9327
tommytuneman@aol.com

Proposal No.:   701-1002-01

Client: Ms. Melody Sweetnote
Address: 14 See Sharp Lane
                  Be Flat, Arkansas, 22222
                  (555)-123-4567

Date: 10/11/2002

Tuneman Productions is proud to offer a recording package to include tracking and mixing of your band, The Sweetnotes. Our service shall include:

- Up to 40 hours of tracking time
- Up to 15 hours of mixing time
- The use of any in-house musical equipment to enhance recording
- Tracking on the ADAT format with new tapes
- Engineer
- Acceptable, for-hire lead guitar player; 6 hours maximum
- 10 CD copies of the final mix down

Package Price: $3,475.00

Terms: **$1,500.00** upon acceptance of this offer;
                  $1,500.00 upon completion of 25 hours of tracking;
                  $475.00 due upon delivery of the final CD mixes.

Expiration: This offer is valid for 30 days from the date of this proposal.

We appreciate the opportunity to offer our services, and hope that we may be favored with your business.

Sincerely,

Tom Volinchak
President, Tuneman Productions

2. Follow-Up Letters

A follow-up letter is an excellent way to demonstrate to your prospects and clients that you care about their projects. Use it to remind a client of upcoming sessions, or as a reminder that payment is due. The follow-up is also a great way to break the ice with a prospect who has not yet responded to your last proposal, as well as an effective way to drum up business from a past client.

I've found that during a typical recording session, issues that directly impact subsequent sessions, project billing or scheduling, and the studio owner's ability to conduct business smoothly often come up. At times, you will find that you are the only one who remembers the details. The bass player who tells everyone, "Yeah, I'll bring the congas next Tuesday," is much more likely to do so if he receives a follow-up reminder letter before that date. A short, hand-written note and a postage stamp are less costly than a lost session.

Think of follow-up letters as vehicles to support your business, which keeps your patrons moving forward according to plan. At first—especially to those of you who have been seat-of-your-pants operators—this will seem like a lot of work. But once you get into the habit of staying on top of your business, the noticeable decline in missed appointments and unprepared clients will astound you.

Here is a typical follow-up letter that could be used in conjunction with the closing of the proposal we issued to Melody Sweetnote in the previous example (notice the reference to the original proposal, and its expiration date, for her convenience). Since I know, from my notes on our initial conversation, that she is concerned about finishing the project on time, I have a legitimate reason to send the following:

Tuneman Productions
101 Riverview Drive, Suite 101
Memphis, TN 38103
(901) 579-9327
tommytuneman@aol.com

October 28, 2002

Ms. Melody Sweetnote
14 See Sharp Lane
Be Flat, Arkansas, 22222

RE: PROPOSAL # 701-1002-01; Expiration date: 11/10/02

Dear Melody,

I am writing to follow up on our discussions about your recording project. The last time we spoke, you mentioned that it was imperative that the tracking be finished by February 2, 2003. I wanted to let you know that we have been booking quite a lot of work at the studio, and available time slots are being reserved fast.

I am still eager to help you with your project, so I will call you on the morning of Monday, November 4, 2002 to discuss your plan for getting into the studio. Please feel free to call me at (901) 579-9327 if you have any questions before then.

Sincerely,

Tom Volinchak
President, Tuneman Productions.

3. Contracts

A simple, friendly, and well-thought-out recording contract can make the difference between a profitable session and a nightmare. I rarely, if ever, perform work without a contract—even for simple tracking jobs. I think you'll find that contracts provide a common point of reference and can save you from many of the pitfalls that confound studio owners.

One of the most frustrating things in this business is when bands and artists fail to show up for scheduled sessions. When a client doesn't show up on schedule, you lose the money that you would have billed for that time; and you can't just call another billable client on the spur of the moment to fill that space. Your contract should specify that missed sessions will be billed at the standard hourly rate. To cement the deal, require an up-front deposit at the contract signing (and stated on the contract) so that you can deduct the cost of any missed sessions from that. Even if a customer is working with you on an hourly rate, call for a retainer/deposit that is refundable after the project is completed. Do not let the client use that deposit to pay for session time; that deposit serves as your security.

Some essential items to include in your contracts:

- Client tracking number, using the same date and numbering system used for your proposal
- Recording format to be used
- Ancillary and/or rental equipment details
- Specific services provided (i.e., tracking, mixing, mastering, etc.)
- Costs and details regarding hired musicians/vocalists
- Format (CD, cassette, etc.) and number of units of finished product
- Licensing issues (publishing, copyright, etc.)
- Start date
- Completion date, if it impacts your pricing
- Refund policies
- Smoking and drinking policy

The following is an example of a typical contract:

Tuneman Productions
101 Riverview Drive, Suite 101
Memphis, TN 38103
(901) 579-9327
tommytuneman@aol.com

Contract No.: 701-1002-01

This document represents an agreement between **Tuneman Productions**, and **Melody Sweetnote** (Client), for the recording of full-length CD project (12 tracks).

Services provided by Tuneman Productions shall include:

- 40 hours of tracking time
- 15 hours of mixing time
- Tracking on ADAT format
- Mixing to DAT format
- 10 CD units of final mix
- 6 hours of guitar work from Mr. Matt Twang; additional hours to be billed at $75.00/hour
- Use of the studio Korg Triton, Yamaha drum set, and BOSS beat machines
- All masters to be the property of Melody Sweetnote

Please note that the accumulated cost of any scheduled session hours missed prior to the commencement of recording session without 72-hour advance notice will be deducted from deposit amount stated below (due upon acceptance of contract). The accumulated cost of any scheduled recording session hours missed after the commencement of sessions will be added to the total cost stated below, and billed accordingly or collected immediately, at the discretion of Tuneman Productions. Recording sessions are recognized as beginning exactly at the time stated below.

Session time is consumed in 1/4-hour increments (a session beginning at 10 A.M. and ending at 1:13 P.M. would be billed at 3 hours).

Client shall assume responsibility for damage to studio equipment incurred by non-recording usage.

**Session Start
Date:** Initial session to begin on Wednesday, December 22, 2002 at 9:00 A.M.

Terms: **$1,500.00** upon acceptance of this contract;

$1,500.00 upon completion of 30 hours of tracking;

$475.00 plus any additional fees incurred due to unapproved session cancellations or additional hired services, upon delivery of the final mixes and master tapes.

We look forward to making your recording experience a successful and enjoyable one.

_____ Date _____
Authorized Agent, Tuneman Productions

_____ Date _____
Client or Authorized Client Representative

4 Tracking Sheets

Since the early days of the music industry, recording engineers have used *tracking sheets* to document all activities in their sessions. Simply stated, a tracking sheet tells which instruments are recorded on which tracks. Their accurate application is essential to maintaining the quality of your recordings. Take it from those more experienced—an accurate tracking sheet makes mix-down a whole lot easier than if one has to sift through 48 tracks to determine where things are.

Most manufacturers of recording equipment provide their own tracking sheets, which allow for the tracking of factors like fader and pan settings, and provide space for you to describe which instrument is recorded on each track. If you purchase used equipment, contact the manufacturer for a copy of their standard tracking sheet.

TRACKING TIP! *Make note of the specific mics used in each session, and their respective distances and placements from the vocalist or instrument. These invaluable factors are not usually noted on the standard sheets, but documenting this will help you to recapture that magic sound, should your artists record more material on a future date. In addition, I recommend that you also note compression and pre-amp settings, which will make punching-in later much easier. Other things to note: specific guitar amp settings, and stomp box particulars.*

In your travels as a studio owner, you're likely to encounter artists who love your demo or one of your recordings. With efficient recordkeeping, you can boast of your ability to duplicate exactly for them your trademark sound. There are no strict rules for building the perfect tracking sheet, but the more data you note, the more useful the tracking sheets will be for you.

MONEY, MONEY, MONEY, MONEY, MONEY!

1. Invoices and Receipts

I know many studio owners who try to operate on a cash basis, but I can tell you first-hand that it doesn't work. It's tricky, financially unwise from a tax perspective, and burdensome. As your business grows, it will become a challenge to keep track of who owes you money and who doesn't unless you have a decent billing system. Use invoices and receipts to keep a tight reign on your finances. At a minimum, I strongly urge you to get one of the simple, easy-to-use, widely available software programs like Quicken to track your finances. It's essential that you make an appointment with a professional accountant to get started.

SALES TIP! *If you award a client a discount, be certain to record it on your billing paperwork and on that client's receipt—both for your record keeping, and also to remind the client of what a great deal you offered. For instance, if for some reason you decide to accept $800.00 for your work instead of the $1,000.00 quoted, document your generosity. Don't just give the customer a receipt for $800.00; instead, present a receipt for $1,000.00 that clearly shows the discount of $200.00 and the new net payment due of only $800.00. Don't think this makes a difference? Just look at the two invoice examples that follow. Notice the potentially positive psychological impact to be made with second invoice, versus the first:*

<u>*Invoice Example 1:*</u>

Tuneman Productions
101 Riverview Drive, Suite 101
Memphis, TN 38103
(901) 579-9327
tommytuneman@aol.com

INVOICE # 817-1108-03

Quantity	Description		Price
1	45 Hour recording session, mixing session, complete with master tapes		$800.00
		Tax	$ 72.00
		Total	$872.00
		PAID	**$872.00**
		BALANCE DUE	-0-

<u>*Invoice Example 2:*</u>

Tuneman Productions
101 Riverview Drive, Suite 101
Memphis, TN 38103
(901) 579-9327
tommytuneman@aol.com

INVOICE # 817-1108-03

Quantity	Description		Price
1	45 Hour recording session, mixing session complete with master tapes		$1,000.00
	* **Repeat Customer Discount**		**$ (200.00)**
		Subtotal	$ 800.00
		Tax	$ 72.00
		Total	$872.00
		PAID	**$872.00**
		BALANCE DUE	-0-

Somewhere down the line, this customer may record another project with you, and when negotiating with him or her then, you can always pull out this invoice copy revisit the good relationship that the two of you enjoyed the first time around. *Good bookkeeping and great relationships are as essential to your success as your technical ability is.*

2. Pricing Strategies

Effective and consistent pricing strategies are absolute necessities for both your peace of mind, and for your ability to carry out day-to-day business. To operate efficiently you must be able to quickly analyze projects and price them in a manner that both delights the customer and supplies you with adequate revenue.

Unless you are new to this industry, you're probably aware of the many home and part-time studios that offer down-and-dirty, lowball pricing to artists. I have seen recording rates from such studios as low as $15–$20 per hour. If you are a kid operating out of your parents' basement, these rates are cool. If you want your business to be your livelihood, they are suicidal.

So how do you offer a great service and compete with these low-rate studios? Well, actually, you don't! Do you really want to do business with people who are looking for a $15/hour studio? How serious can an artist be about his or her music if recording at what could be the Tone Deaf Academy for Bad Sound Production?

If you have dreams of adding a Neumann to your equipment arsenal, if you fantasize about expanding your outboard gear, if you imagine yourself recording radio hits, you need to market to clients, who, like you, have sincere aspirations for their careers and who, like you, seek out excellence in their associates.

Your business will grow based on clients who pay your rate and walk away happy. These clients will come back to record again, and they will serve as your ambassadors by bringing new clients to your door. While I wouldn't tell you to turn your nose up at the artists who use the cut-rate studios (some of those clients will graduate and seek better services as their careers develop), I will remind you that part of the task in growing your studio is to become an educator and a standard-bearer in the recording community. You can do yourself and the industry a service by identifying exactly what your core principles in recording are, and then to stand by them in your offerings.

During the early days of your operation, when there is nobody knocking at your door, you will be strongly tempted to leap into the cut-rate arena and capture the "el cheapo" clients. In my early studio days, I did the same thing for a short while. The instinct to survive is strong, I confess. However, take it from someone who has been there: once you dip into the bargain basement arena, the el cheapos will quickly consume your entire existence, and you will have very little time left to cultivate profitable clients.

When business is slow, think about what successful major corporations do in tough economic times: they may offer slight discounts, but they focus on enticing sluggish buyers with value-added services and attractive financing strategies that keep sales moving and margins high. Would bargain basement customers pay your higher rate if you offered them 90 days to pay off their balance? It's worth a shot!

A good pricing strategy will save you from poverty. Focus on value-added selling techniques whenever possible and you won't have to compete with the sharks. What else can you offer your clients that they'll find valuable, but won't cost you too much in time or other expenses?

Perhaps you can offer your customers a spot on a "local writers night" talent showcase that you sponsor. Other ideas might be to help get local airplay through personal contacts, or maybe you can offer them five free CDs. Get creative and draw from all those resources that make you the special individual you are. Pull out all the stops!

3. Competitive Hourly Rates

A competitive hourly rate will be the staple of your pricing strategy—not because you are going to sell based on price (it is my sworn duty to get you away from selling on an hourly rate!), but because that's how everybody else on the block is operating. I want you to use your hourly rate as a standard tool so that your prospects will see right off the bat how competitive you are.

The best way to set your standard hourly rate is to survey similarly equipped, successful studios within a 200-mile radius. Try to compare apples to apples; don't expect to command the same price as a studio offering a Neve Console when you have a Mackie 4-bus. On the other hand, if you have a Mackie, don't lower your rates to match the studio offering a Yamaha MT8-X cassette system. Use common sense! If studios similar to yours are in the $35–$55 per hour range, shoot for the higher end without being the most expensive. In this example, I would have settled on $50 per hour.

4. Package Pricing

The best way to prevent clients from comparing your hourly rates to that of other studios is to offer package pricing. If presented properly, package pricing can yield more profits than standard hourly pricing.

This strategy takes the guesswork out of budgeting for the artist—which is a great selling point! *When you quote a package price, the artist knows exactly what it will cost to complete the project*. This is a huge benefit since nothing is worse for a band than beginning a CD project, running through its budget too soon, and having to shelve it for months until they can afford to finish.

Package pricing also frees your clients from the distraction of watching the clock—another terrific selling point. Who performs their best while watching their $70 hour ticking away? Explain to your prospects that when they buy a package deal from you, their only focus will be getting their music recorded. This way the stress is on you, not them, to get it right.

Package pricing places the onus of efficiency on the engineer and studio. To make this technique work, you must be set up and ready to go when the artists arrive to record. *Using this strategy gives the studio a commercial advantage, because most artists don't know how long their project will take to complete*. An astute studio owner should be able to make good assessments. At first, you may miscalculate a few package deals and work more cheaply than you want to, but eventually, you will master the strategy and start turning nice profits. Most importantly, you will get jobs, keep working, and eliminate the competition.

Here is an example of how package pricing worked for me: a four-piece rock band came to my studio to record an eight-song CD, which they thought that they could record in twenty-five hours. Another studio quoted them a rate of $35/hour.

My approach was to first to go over all the details of what the band wanted to accomplish, get them comfortable with my studio and abilities, and talk about the concept of package pricing. That accomplished, I pointed out that my competitor didn't account for mixing or normalization costs, which could take another fifteen hours. The band acknowledged and agreed with these points.

With much discussion, everyone felt that forty total hours (based on the other studio's projections) was what it would take to complete the project. Since they were using $35/hour as their source of comparison, I felt comfortable in assuming that this band was prepared to spend a total of $1,400 on the recording.

I knew that the band was tight and that my studio was efficient, and I believed that I could get this band tracked in about ten hours, and probably mixed and normalized in another ten.

My proposal to them included tracking, mixing (up to two mixes), normalization, ten CDs, and up to fifty hours of recording for a grand total of $1,350. Based on experience, I was confident that it wouldn't take fifty hours to complete this project, but it gave the client a real sense of comfort knowing that I would give them ten more hours of service (if necessary) for less money than the cut-rate studio.

Of course, if the band did take fifty hours to finish I would be the loser—but I'd still have the business and experience for devising my future pricing scheme. Knowing your business is tantamount to your success with package pricing.

As it turned out, I finished this particular project in twenty-two hours, which netted me a nifty average rate of $61.36 per hour. The customers were comfortable and at ease in my studio, so they never had reason to count hours. Over the next two years, these guys recorded with me three more times, and never again asked for an hourly rate quote.

SALES TIP! *Studios operating on an hourly rate very often convince prospects that a project is going to take more time than it actually should. The reason is clear; on an hourly rate, the studio makes more money on longer projects. Use this knowledge in your battle to beat the bargain-basement studios. Remember: thirty hours at $25/hour costs a lot more overall than twelve hours at $50/hour. If you are sure that you can complete the project in twelve, then go for it! Allow the customer a maximum of thirty hours—equal to the competitor's offer—but charge a package price based on the twelve that you know it will take. Use this technique properly and you will leave your competitors baffled.*

5. Quick Packages

In chapter 4, I listed some alternative places to look for clients, such as record stores and songwriter associations. Offering *quick packages* will help you sell to such prospects. With a tri-fold brochure or possibly a CD demo, you could detail everything these clients would ever need to know about doing business with you. You'll find that quick packages save time, money, effort, and are an easy way to communicate your services.

For example, you could offer something like this to karaoke singers:

- Professional, three-song recording including producer/engineer
- State-of-the-art digital recording
- 1,500 songs to choose from, or the option of providing own
- Digital pitch correction and vocal enhancement
- Ten CD copies, complete with cases and labels

   Total Package...$ 275.00

The effectiveness of this tool becomes clear when you compare the simplicity of offering a straightforward $275.00 package, as opposed to trying to explain and justify your $50/hour rate to the nontraditional customer who really does not understand the recording industry.

Promotional Tools

1. Brochures

You can have one tri-fold brochure for all of your nontraditional clients, or you can create a separate flyer for each type, but it's important to develop a mechanism for selling that requires the least amount of administrative effort.

A brochure is an excellent vehicle for:

- Showcasing your impressive recording credentials
- Listing your equipment and capabilities
- Advertising special package deals for the month
- Announcing free seminars or open house events
- Sending out a fact-finding questionnaire to build your database

Also consider including a technical tip or two to help aspiring artists make better music. It's an excellent way to set you apart from the competition and establish yourself as the resident recording expert. If you can come up with a series of tips (and make it clear that each one is part of a series), you can get people to pick up your brochure repeatedly. Since you don't know when someone will be ready to sign on the dotted line and record, it helps to be in touch over time. (Be sure to highlight the tip number on the front page of the brochure to alert the reader to a new tip!)

In addition to handing out brochures to your visitors, you can leave some at music stores, record stores, club bulletin boards, and just about anywhere people do business. Create an email version that you can access whenever you get a new contact. If you use AOL, Yahoo!, or another Internet services that requires registration and offers member profiles, make sure that you create a profile that highlights your business. Offer a free brochure including recording tips, and you will be surprised at how many requests you get from people searching the member directory for experts and advice!

2. Email

This wonderful form of communication must be a basic staple of your operation. Email is useful to:

- Send proposals
- Confirm appointments
- Contact new clients
- Keep in touch with developing projects
- Get updates on equipment repairs
- Send out notices of monthly studio specials

Today, there is no excuse to be without email—it's simple, easy to acquire, and inexpensive. Your email address should be something that is easy to remember, and has a topical connection to your business. If you don't already have one, get a free email account at Yahoo! or MSN Hotmail. Contracting with a major Internet provider is more secure because there is less of a chance your email supplier will go out of business—leaving you high and dry without a link to your customers.

Choose a screen name dedicated to your business, and one that uses your business name, if possible. For example:

BigRedStudios@yahoo.com or BigRedStudios@AOL.com

Ultimately, a growing business needs its own domain name with a dedicated email address that can serve multiple users. This is the most professional way to conduct business, and it's growing cheaper everyday. Contact Yahoo!, AOL, MSN, or others and they'll be happy to set you up with your own domain for nominal fees. An example of a business domain name:

John@BigRedStudios.com

Good email services allow you to store, sort, and categorize files according to your particular needs. You can store individual addresses and group mailing lists of thousands of clients and prospects. There are even mass mailing programs that allow you to capture unlimited numbers of new names and add them to your mailing lists. Emails are also a wonderfully simple way to document your conversations. Regardless of the weather, your mood, the time, the season, or even the economy, email will serve you and allow you to move your business forward. Importantly, email is free and instantaneous. Just remember to link or attach key communications you have with customers to their files.

3. Newsletters

If you have the time and resources, issuing a regular newsletter to past clients and new prospects can be an excellent way to cultivate business and keep public interest in your studio at peak levels. Newsletters can include some of the same kind of information found in your brochure but can be expanded to list recent bands and projects that you have worked on. A newsletter can invite the public to one of your seminars, list where all the local bands are playing, or include other relevant information your customer base might be interested in.

If you decide to publish your own newsletter, you must find ways to keep mailing and printing costs in line, which can quickly become prohibitive. The effort to produce and distribute a regular publication can be quite time-consuming, so find ways to standardize the process and enlist the help of friends, colleagues, and interns. Email is a cheaper way to go if you have the contact email list to support it. You will find that email lists can be the perfect vehicles to launch your own newsletter.

As with media advertising, I advise that a newsletter include some type of free offer or special discount. That way you can gauge how well the publication is doing based on the response to your special offer.

4. Your Website

An effective website is one of the most important tools you will ever use in growing your business. It's simply inexcusable not to have a website for your studio.

A website can:

- Offer audio samples of your work
- Provide guidance and education to the recording public
- Supply directions to your studio
- List standard pricing schedules
- Describe your studio's features and benefits
- Announce special events and promotions
- Provide links to the websites of artists who have recorded with you, or other credentials and recommendations

A website can look like a major Hollywood movie production complete with every bell and whistle available. However, somewhere along the line, time, budget, and practicality are going to govern the choices you make when building it. Opinions will vary on what constitutes the better websites, and making your choices can appear confusing; but simple logic focused on the main selling points of your studio will help you arrive at your perfect website quickly and economically.

If possible, purchase the domain name of your business. Per the above domain name example, it would mean registering the name BigRedStudios.com. For just a hundred dollars or less, you can register a domain name and protect your exclusive use of any name available, provided it's not already taken and you can justify your rights to it should there ever be a dispute. Since dot-coms are running out of availabilities, you should also register under dot-net (i.e., BigRedStudios.net), but use this address to redirect users to the main dot-com site. This is important when listing your website with the search engines. Dot-com addresses have been the standard for so long that it's critical you secure one for your business—even if it means a slight adjustment to the business name you had intended to use.

NOTE: *You must have clear rights to the name you want to use. If you tried to secure "CocaCola.com," for example, even if it were available, you would not have rights to it. Coca Cola would easily secure the domain away from you because they have all versions of their name trademarked for other usages.*

Be practical and above-board with your selections. Registering your name as a state corporation runs $150 or less; the fee for a Federal Trademark runs around $325.

Overall, websites that are visually pleasing and easy to navigate are best. Keep in mind that complex visuals, sounds, and intricate dissolves, etc. all slow down the user's download. Resist the temptation to use sound on the home or first page. Studies show that many users will abandon the site rather than wait too long to get what they want. If no one sees your cool graphics or hears your audio file, it doesn't exist! Keep in mind that just a small percentage of Internet users have the latest computer technology and fastest access, so keep it simple!

In addition to listing your address and contact information, your website must offer some tasty, clear pictures of your studio. A combination of pictures showing the studio both empty and filled with people working is a good idea, and a quality shot of you at the helm of your console is always the best choice for a photo centerpiece. Don't skimp! If you are great with photography and feel comfortable taking your own pictures then have at it; but a professional photographer is usually best for the most businesslike website.

Nothing gives prospects a better impression of your abilities than their initial view of your studio, so take the time and care to do this properly. Believe it or not, I have seen website pictures that show alcohol containers, equipment held together with duct tape, and wires trailing all over the studio. These all detract from your professional image.

Use the absolute best scanning technology available to convert your selected photos into the digital world. A digital camera is an easy way to load pictures and send them out, but may not afford the high-quality definition necessary for use in your website. Be certain to check the quality of any photo uploaded to your site. If you have a scanner for standard photos, make sure your scanner is of the best resolution available. If it isn't, pay someone to scan your photos. (Kinko's and other business services can help you with this cheaply and easily.)

The music samples on your website should be topical, short in duration, and always labeled clearly, so the user knows that he or she is selecting an audio track. (Many people are listening to tunes through their computer, so you don't want to crash their system with competing audio links just as they are deciding that yours is the studio for their project!) Think about the potential styles of artists that you serve, then choose music that relates to them. Simplicity is essential. The purpose of your website is to give a prospect a glimpse of your business that entices them to check you out in person. If they have to wait fifteen minutes to download complex musical files, they are not likely to hang around to learn about your studio.

It is a good idea to offer a discount to anyone who books time in your studio as a result of visiting your website. For example, by tracking the number of people who come in asking for the "surfer's discount," you can get a good idea of how effective your website really is at attracting business!

5. The Five Most Important Words on Your Website

Taken with alterations from an article by Nick Usborne of MarketingProfs.com

No. 1: "FREE"

"Free" is an extremely important word in the world of offline marketing, and it is just as important online—maybe more so, because so much marketing online incorporates free offers from the start. For your studio, you could offer the following for free:

- Studio time (i.e., two free karaoke recordings with every five-song package)
- CDs (i.e., five free CDs with every songwriter demo package)
- T-shirt
- Mastering (i.e., free with every project of eight songs or more)

If you have any doubts about whether users of the web are interested in "free," do a quick search on Google. Nick Usborne did, and got *172 million* results! One caveat: many people filter out emails that use the word "free" in their subject lines.

No. 2: "SIGN UP"

Okay, it's two words. The point is that every site should invite visitors to sign up or subscribe to an email program or newsletter. Then you can reach your prospects by email.

People check their email more frequently than they surf the web—much more, in fact. Research shows that the conversion rate of first-time visitors into immediate purchasers is horribly low. Furthermore, the person who bailed after spending a few seconds on your homepage is unlikely to be coming back again any time soon.

So instead of hoping that your visitors will make a purchase on their first visit, concentrate instead on collecting their email addresses by getting them to sign up for your online newsletter or email list.

Caveat: your emails or newsletters had better be good. Good content in their inbox will bring visitors back to your site again and again. Poor content will damage your chances of ever hearing from them again.

No. 3: "BUY"

As has been stressed before, you need to ask for the sale. It is amazing how many sites invest energy into presenting products and services, but fail to invest in tactics to close the sale. Again, conversion rates online are nothing to write home about, so make sure that you actually ask for the sale at the right moment.

Make that "buy" link prominent, both by positioning it close to the image or description of the product or service, and by boosting it with a strong graphic.

The word "buy" is a verb—it instructs people to do something. So make that instruction jump out and grab their attention.

No. 4: "NOW"

"Now" is good; "later" is death. If someone digs deep enough into your site to find the product or service they want, but then only makes a mental note to come back again some other time, you've probably lost that potential customer.

The web is an easy-come and easy-go environment. If you can't get people to act immediately, forget it. So ask people to do things "now." For example:

- Sign up NOW
- Buy NOW
- Tell a friend NOW

Go even further with some incentives:

- Sign up NOW and receive a FREE guide to a successful recording!
- Buy NOW and get 10 FREE CDs!

No 5: "THANK YOU"

Okay, so it's two words again—but it's the thought that counts. When you sign up a subscriber or make a sale—when visitors become customers—your work has just begun. Just because someone signs up for your newsletter does not mean that he or she will actually read it. And just because someone buys your product doesn't mean that he or she won't send it back. You have a relationship to build. The first step in building that relationship is to say, "Thank you." It's courteous. It's the right thing to say.

Maybe this will inspire you to go back to those automated "acknowledgement" emails that you wrote a few years back. Rewrite them; be personal; say, "Thank you."

If you are a website do-it-yourselfer, several providers will offer you free (or nearly free) web space and construction tools to get your show started. Some of the better free sources are:

- http://free.prohosting.com
- www.geocities.com
- www.freeservers.com
- www.dreamwater.com
- www.freewebspace.com
- www.freewebspace.net

Also, www.100best-free-web-space.com will provide you with one hundred sources of free web space in addition to those already listed.

If you can afford to hire a professional to create and manage your website, both the site and your business will benefit. A good website needs to be updated and maintained from time to time to keep it fresh. Occasionally, technical problems will arise that will need attention, so get some technical help lined up. Keep in mind that you intend to have a successful studio, which means you'll be busy marketing, selling, recording, and polishing all your future award-winning projects, leaving you no time to function also as webmaster. Do yourself a favor; hire a pro.

chapter 5
Adding Value to Your Business

No matter what products and services a company offers, they operate on one of two principles: high volume/low margin (such as Wal-Mart or Toys R Us), or the low volume/high margin (such as Mercedes Benz or Cartier). Note that all of these companies offer supreme service and quality products regardless of their selling strategies.

One of the big challenges you'll face in the studio business is the constant pressure to submit to *downward pricing*—the lowering of your prices—in order to compete with the many new, personal and project studios popping up everywhere. Advances in technology have made it easy to build small, efficient studios on a surprisingly small budget. Thus, competition for new clients is growing fiercer by the minute, and the most common reaction of studio owners is to lower prices. However, lower prices don't always equal more business volume, and can translate into minimal profits.

Downward-pricing pressure is a reality, but you still need to earn a living, keep up with advancing technology, maintain your equipment, and seek additional training from time to time. Offering cut-rate prices may get you through a tough month or two, but it is not a sound strategy for the long haul. Successful businesses command a fair price for their products and services; studio owners should expect to do the same.

The key to combating downward-pricing pressure is in offering *value-added* products and services. Simply defined, a value-added item is anything that offers the buyer additional benefits over and above that offered by the competition. In the automobile business, a value-added offer might be a 60,000-mile warranty or roadside emergency assistance. In the cereal business, it may be a free toy inside the box. In the electronics business, it may be a lifetime of free software upgrades. Value-added products and services are those things that differentiate you from your competitors, and allow you to command a fair price for your work.

Let's look at some effective value-added benefits that you can offer your clients:

Creature Comforts

Sometimes a client chooses a studio because the creature comforts offered make it a convenient and friendly place to work. Often, these benefits have nothing to do with the recording advantages at all. For instance, having a few toys, or coloring books and crayons available for the kiddies will make your studio attractive to artistic parents. A little side room and a baby gate to keep kids out of the middle of things might just make you the talk of the town! That same room can also double as a lounge when equipped with a comfortable couch and TV for artists waiting for their turns in the booth.

Your clients will appreciate the use of a telephone. Even in this age of cell phones, it's nice to offer privacy for that artist who needs to make a personal call. His and hers restrooms are nice, but if you only have room for one washroom, make sure it is spotless and offers adequate privacy. Soap, paper towels, proper ventilation, and a functioning, locking door are absolute musts. All that and a pot of fresh coffee and/or a regular supply of soft drinks can give your studio a homey feel. Remember, artists are people too. The more comfortable your patrons are, the happier they will be with your services. Happy clients make great ambassadors for your studio.

Another great way to add value and offer convenience to your clients is to hire an apprentice or assistant. Doing so will allow you to offer clients, or their guests or spouses, transportation to the local shopping mall or movie house during long sessions. Assistants can also serve as "runners," by running errands or going out for items needed by the artists, guests, or recording staff, allowing them to continuing their session uninterrupted. (In addition, an assistant can help with studio chores and clean up, as well as assist you with your marketing efforts by delivering flyers, or even doing some telemarketing for you.)

TIP! *In the early stages of your studio development, the workload may get intense enough that at times you need help. At the same time, your budget may not afford you the ability to hire an assistant. One of the things that worked famously for me was offering training apprenticeships to local university students who were interested in the recording industry. If you have a university-based recording school near your studio, explore with them the possibility of a student apprentice. Universities are sometimes willing to give course credit for such work, which supplies you with a long line of eager students willing to offer their time and energy to learn a bit more about an industry they love.*

Artist Comforts

Keep them in tune! It's amazing how many musicians will show up for a session without an electronic tuner. My studios have rack-mounted digital units that can be read from any recording booth. When a particular player questions his or her tuning, I patch him or her into the tuner to check things out. (After each song, I like to be certain everyone was dead-on so we don't waste time. Fortunately, I've always enjoyed a reputation for producing a sweet marriage of all the instruments, and that has brought me business.)

Musicians often get to a session without back-up strings, batteries, patch cords, picks, reeds, capos, slides, or other accessories they really need. You can offer these items for sale at a slightly higher price than the local music stores, and find that your clients will gladly pay the small markup while appreciating the session-saving convenience. I'm not advocating that you become a music retailer, but you can win major points by saving a player from having to leave a session to hit the local music shop, or worse, needing to reschedule a session because all the retail shops are closed.

My local music store has always been cooperative in letting me keep a small supply of such accessories on consignment. The stuff sells, and adds to my revenue. After regular business hours, I sometimes get drop-in artists from other studios looking to fill their late night accessory needs!

Music Industry Information

People usually record to make the world aware of their work. By establishing your studio as a source of music business information, you will capture the lasting attention of your intended audience. This information can include trade magazines, articles about new music legislation and technology, record label press releases, listings of artists actively seeking new material, local music scene news, or anything else that might appeal to a recording artist. If your town offers one of those local music scene newspapers, make sure you have a few of the latest editions available. Up-to-date industry information is a great little addition to the services you offer.

Client Performances

A cool way to win the confidence of a new prospect, grow their respect, and lock them into your services is to listen to them play in their live environment before you record them. In addition, hearing a band perform before recording can give you some good direction technically. It allows you to better prepare for such things as noisy amplifiers, overplaying guitarists, squeaky drum sets and out of tune vocalists. Taking the time to hear a band live will not only help your sessions run more smoothly, it will also establish you as a studio owner who actually is involved with his clients. Both of these factors will translate into profits and successful long-term relationships.

Post-Production Services

Doesn't it seem that everyone is offering post-production services—artwork, logo design, and retail-ready CDs? It might strike you as a great value-added service to offer these items to your clients, but doing so presents some challenges, so be careful.

There are several economically priced pieces of equipment on the market if you're doing a short production run of disks for your clients. On the other hand, for true retail packaging—especially in quantities of 250 pieces or more—it's next to impossible to compete with the major production houses. Many artists already know about these mega-operations because of big ads in the music industry trades. These artists are not likely to ask for your assistance in getting their work duplicated and packaged.

Other artists however, will ask you to quote a price for these post-production services. If you do decide to jump into any of these arenas, there are a couple ways to go about it—although they require that you secure the services of an established CD printer/packager, and then make your money on top of their fee. A couple of such options for you to explore are:

- Seek out reliable, low-priced suppliers, and then tack on an additional 10–20% in commission for themselves.
- Seek production houses that pay a direct commission to any studio sending business their way. The more CD jobs that you refer, the more generous they can be with the commission they pay you.

Over the years, I have used a combination of both approaches. For those clients with significant graphic requirements because they wanted a truly retail-ready package with a major label look, I referred them to pros such as Discmakers. This company has handled all of my clients' needs, and has paid me a 5% commission for the referral. On less demanding clients' works, I do some of the text copy, layout, and graphics, and then send the package out to one of the discount houses for duplication and packaging. I mark the project up to a price close to what the big houses charge, and generally earn an extra couple of hundred bucks on an order of 1,000 CDs.

A word of caution: offering post-production services carries a greater risk in your having an unsatisfactory product if you go with the bargain-basement services. My rule of thumb has always been to offer these types of services as value-added tools, and perhaps make a few dollars in the process. Trying to capitalize overzealously on post-production services can be disastrous when you encounter one of those too-good-to-be-true bargain companies, who are famous for shoddy workmanship and substandard service. For example, you may order and pay for 1,000 packaged CDs, but only receive 788; and out of those, some may even be blank.

Ultimately, unless you are willing to devote yourself to the post-production end of the studio business, you are not going to make a whole lot of your money on these ancillary services. It helps to be prepared with quality contacts for that occasional client who wants you to provide them with full service. Just be careful when you choose your vendors.

Encoding

There is a new development in the music industry, which will have an immediate and dramatic impact on the CD duplicating companies, and which can increase the revenue streams of individual studio owners if used aggressively. The process is called *encoding*.

To combat digital song thievery on the Internet, the major record labels have invested in researching the best ways to alter their CDs so that unlawful duplication of any kind is impossible. Encoding devices remove minute sections from recordings. The removal of this material is inaudible to the human ear, but is confounding to a computer attempting to read and copy a CD. Reportedly, some encoding machines can actually destroy the CD writer of an unlicensed copier. Fortunately, this version of the technology isn't likely to be adopted.

Encoding represents an interesting moneymaking proposition for the bold individual studio owner. Should this new toy become an economically priced option, a savvy studio pro will be able to encode the final mixes delivered to a client while retaining the non-encoded master. In this scenario, the studio could actually charge a fee if the client wanted to personally seek out his own CD duplicator with the final mixes.

This practice wouldn't exactly be a way to make clients happy, and I would never recommend it; but it certainly gives rise to discussions about a potentially new performance/mechanical/duplication royalty license for studio owners, doesn't it? The legalities involved have yet to be tested, but stay tuned as these issues continue to be resolved!

Publishing

While publishing is not for everyone, it is a potential value-added service that I feel is worth a look. The primary function of a publisher is to collect royalties from the performance of an artist's work. These royalties are collected from the performance rights organization with which the music and/or artist is registered. Performance royalties are assessed on performances from a variety of places including radio, TV, jukebox play, live music venues, karaoke bars, bowling alleys, retail shops, trade shows, and even funeral homes.

Operating a publishing company as part of your services will enable you to provide several important benefits to your clients:

- If your clients write their own music, you can guide them in the protection of their art, while reaping financial benefits from any performance of their material.

- Outside writers will send you material for consideration. Attracting new artists to your studio is a lot easier when you can also offer them a catalog of original songs, to which you have rights, for their projects.

- It can build your reputation as a music expert if any of the artists you record hit the big time with material that you published.

Naturally, most songwriters will expect you to get their material recorded by nationally recognized artists. If these works get payable airplay, you, as the publisher, have the legal obligation to audit the airplay, compare the royalties to those paid for similar performances by the competing performance rights organizations (PROs), and administer the payments to the authors of those songs. However, as a publisher, you would also share in the royalties generated by that music.

For music that attains national exposure, publishing one song can generate enough revenue to make it worth it for you to developing a publishing company. For music played on a limited or regional basis, this same publishing function can rob you of precious studio time.

Not all publishers serve as song promoters. In some modified arrangements, the material is published simply to protect the composer in the event that their music is discovered through the artist's own efforts. Once a piece of music gets played, or another entity (like a label) shows interest, the original publisher can transfer the music to another publisher already equipped for royalty administration, and keep a small percentage of the song ownership for him- or herself.

By offering publishing services to your clients, you increase the value of your service greatly; but it can also burden you with unexpected responsibilities. Before making a decision to add this feature to your services list, it is a good idea to learn more about the legalities and requirements involved.

On its website, SESAC President and COO Bill Velez addresses the question, "What is a performance rights organization?" He states that "... performing rights organizations, such as SESAC, are businesses designed to represent songwriters and publishers and their right to be compensated for having their music performed in public. By securing a license from SESAC, for example, music users (i.e., television and radio stations, auditoriums, restaurants, hotels, theme parks, malls, funeral homes, etc.) can legally play any song in the SESAC repertory. Without a license from a performing rights organization, music users are in danger of copyright infringement."

There are three PROs that offer publishing licenses, and I recommend that you obtain a license from each one of them. Properly licensed, you will be able to record, produce, promote, and distribute the work of any potential artists who come into your studio. For those not familiar with music publishing, each one of the PROs offers information on how to get started as a publisher. Your prospects will appreciate your understanding of this end of the business. The three PROs are:

- **American Society of Composers, Authors, and Publishers (ASCAP)**
  One Lincoln Plaza, New York, NY 10023
  (212) 595-3276
  www.ascap.com

- **Broadcast Music, Inc. (BMI)**
  320 West 57th Street, New York, NY 10019-3790
  (212) 586-2000
  www.bmi.com

- **SESAC**
  55 Music Square East, Nashville, TN 37203
  (615) 320-0055
  www.sesac.com

Music Licensing

You are likely to encounter artists who want to record a work owned by someone else. Set yourself apart from the competition by knowing how to obtain a music license for song usage. The Harry Fox Agency can provide you with all the information you need to learn about obtaining mechanical music licenses:

The Harry Fox Agency
711 Third Avenue, New York, NY 10017
(212) 370-5330
www.harryfox.com

Note: *This website also links you to the National Music Publishers Association, a sister association of the Harry Fox Agency.*

Always try to add value to what you offer. There are countless ways that you can add value, and I hope that the examples cited in this chapter will inspire you to come up with value-added features of your own. Remember that what works in one studio may not work in another. If for instance you have techno-music clients, a groove machine like the Yamaha RS7000 would add a lot of value to your services. That same piece of equipment however, would do nothing for the studio that records mostly country acts. Before adding a product or service, consider the regional habits and artistic needs of your clientele, and understand what equipment will command premium pricing.

chapter 6
Finding New Business

It would be great if everyone who walked through the doors of your studio were a Grammy Award-winner with his or her next winning project in hand. But until the next Britney Spears graces your doorstep, you'll have to generate revenue to pay the bills. If you are able to put your pride aside and look at the marketplace sensibly, you are apt to find a plethora of worthwhile moneymaking opportunities that will fund your desires to follow your musical dreams.

A prudent studio owner should walk away from projects that aren't good for the business; but that owner can't afford to walk away from things because the client doesn't meet some ideal of professionalism or talent. I've seen studio owners turn up their noses at projects that don't feature mainstream, professional musicians or established bands while struggling to meet their overhead. This is not smart business management. For most studio owners, profitability is found outside of the commercial mainstream.

 **Diversify!**

If I could credit one thing for the success of my own studio endeavors, it would be that I *diversified* my client list—acquiring business from virtually every possible market segment. While my competitors were complaining that local bands didn't have any money to finish their projects, I was complaining that there weren't enough hours in the day. While they were whining about the lack of business, I was unhappy because I couldn't find enough help to assist me with all the in-house projects I had. Sure, the bands I worked with had the same kind of financial challenges that other bands had, but while they were trying to get their funds together, I wasn't sitting on my hands. Instead, I was either working on other quick, simple, but paying projects, or I was out drumming up new business.

I always view my studio as a work in progress—attracting projects that can gain notoriety and push my talents to new heights. However, I also want to use my skills to work on other projects that are fun and profitable. By not limiting myself to one particular market segment, my studio has always been hustling and bustling with projects, which not only keep my doors open, but also allow me to hone my skills. That's a lot more than the guy down the street who only records the rock bands that maintain his "artistic integrity" can say.

In the early days of my studio, alternative markets were the staples of my existence. I suggest that you take the time to explore these potential opportunities, as they are wonderful ways for you to generate revenue in a competitive marketplace—revenue that will allow you to keep your doors open when others around you are struggling.

B The Karaoke / Novelty Market

Offering recording services to starry-eyed karaoke singers is simple and rewarding because, unbelievably, karaoke can offer rather nice profits. The key to building this business is in getting to know the DJs and karaoke owners, as they get constant calls from aspiring artists looking for recording studios). Networking with you adds credibility to their range of services, so they will welcome your help. (Plus, as I mentioned in Chapter 5, the karaoke owners will sometimes offer you a page or two of advertising space inside their song-selection books, which is a great way to pick up new business.

If you record their clients, the karaoke owners will usually make their song library available to you for a nominal finder's fee, or assist you in acquiring a small song library of your own, so that you can offer "vanity" or special occasion recordings. Christmas, Valentine's Day, Mother's Day, Father's Day, and other holidays can offer you a great opportunity to capitalize on the novelty recording business. Folks love to record something to celebrate special occasions for friends and loved ones; your karaoke song library will give you the opportunity to offer specials—for a holiday gift, a sweetheart recording their partner's favorite love song, or a kid sending a special message to their grandparents, etc. (Here is a bonus: occasionally, such business may uncover that rare singer who can help you in the studio with demos; I always welcome a new vocalist who can add diversity to my offerings.)

TIP! *Always remember to check the mechanical licensing disclaimer on the material that you are re-recording. These fees are usually nominal, but must be paid! (See Chapter 5, "Music Licensing.")*

Record Stores

I send out flyers to record stores offering clean up, enhancement, and the transfer of scratchy records onto cassette or CD. You would be amazed at how many people have old records that they would love to be able to use on their modern, high-tech stereo systems. Marketed properly, you can get a lot of mileage out of a HUSH noise reduction system and a BBE Sonic Maximizer. The record shops are more than happy to recommend me to their customers, and many of them actually display my flyers in their shops.

Bridal Shops and Wedding Planner Services

This one won't apply to every studio, but exploring niche markets can be very profitable for you. For example, bridal shops and wedding planner services are in the business of serving brides-to-be every day—helping them put together the perfect wedding—which might include custom recordings! Frequently, friends or family members want to sing a sentimental song at a wedding reception or ceremony. If the band or organist doesn't know the selection desired, a studio that performs vocal reduction/removal on existing recordings can come in quite handy.

There is a variety of equipment available to do vocal reductions, which may be an unused feature of a product you already have in-house. (In my own case, the vocal remover offered by the effects card in my Roland VS-1680 has paid for the cost of the entire system.) If you currently have established karaoke contacts, or have built your own sound library, you can offer personalized studio recordings to commemorate a wedding without the need for a vocal reduction unit.

With a well-stocked supply of standard tunes sequenced as MIDI files, you can record singers and provide back up. If you are an accomplished player and arranger, it might be economical for you to arrange, perform, and sequence the desired songs yourself. Whatever your capabilities, bridal shops and wedding planner services can be excellent referral services.

Charitable Compilations

While I am not a huge fan of new artist compilation CDs, I have found a great marketplace in putting together projects for charitable or nonprofit organizations such as churches, school bands, community theatres, and other music-oriented clubs. Many of these institutions have wonderful music that they are proud of and want to share with others. A spot on a CD compilation gives these groups an economical way to get notoriety for their music, and raise funds for other worthwhile projects.

Compilations consist of works by organizations that were offered a spot on the promotional CD for a fee. For argument's sake, let's say that fee is $1,750. Fifteen participants on the project would translate into gross revenue of $26,250. In return for the fee, each participant would be recorded professionally, and given 250 CDs to sell at fundraisers or otherwise for profit. Additional CDs over the 250 would be offered to participants at a nominal charge of, say, $3.50 each.

If you are able to get local radio play and promotion for these projects, your value as a producer and studio entity can rise like a rocket. Holidays are an excellent time to release compilations, and local record shops are usually eager to place local music on their shelves for sale. The most attractive part of these projects is that they provide a nice return on investment for everyone.

F Bumper Tunes and Theme Songs

If you have the musical talent, you can try your hand at writing a few catchy *bumper tunes*—music played during the segue of a commercial break back to the DJ—for popular radio personalities, which will garner you free radio publicity, referrals, and sometimes the business of other DJs for similar work. Personalization works best when you present tunes to the radio show hosts. At most, bumpers can be true moneymakers if sold properly. At least, you will make some very good contacts in your community.

In addition to bumper music, many DJs, politicians, high school teams, and other professional organizations would love to have a theme song that identifies their professional personas. Ego is a wonderful thing when it compels someone to pay you for your work; and while it's unlikely anyone will make a fortune producing personalized tunes, it sure doesn't hurt to have a local celebrity using your creation as his or her theme song!

G Songwriter Organizations

Songwriters are not necessarily accomplished musicians or producers. Sometimes a cleverly produced, cleanly recorded demo can make the difference in whether a writer gets a song cut or not. Songwriter groups are always open to guest speakers, so take the opportunity to meet local writers or attend their workshops. One of my most effective selling tools was a simple cassette of before-and-after demos that I did for a local writer. The "before" example featured an unintentionally distorted acoustic guitar, and a likewise distorted, flat, vocal performance. The "after" example was a clean, slick, full-band demo with a hot vocal interpretation. Writers love to hear their work professionally polished, and a good before-and-after comparison is a great way to sell your services and build repeat business.

Graphic Illustrators

I once met a woman who owned a graphics illustrating company that did a lot of spectacular 3-D animation for medical, industrial, and criminal law suits. Typically, she would create beautiful animations—comparable to the stuff we see in the movies—but she was using run-of-the-mill, canned music to enhance her work. After visiting her studio, I offered to compose custom music for a 2 1/2-minute factory explosion animation that she had just completed; and we have been working together ever since. Other graphics illustrator contacts came my way on her referral, too.

There are multitudes of graphics illustrators for virtually everything from corporate training films to science and medical films, from animation to documentary; and most need music.

Trade Shows

Do not overlook industry trade shows as a client source. You might find, as I have, that you can get work assembling clever theme compilation CDs to go along with the various presentations being made at events.

A few years ago, a postal worker/songwriter friend of mine was asked to come up with a catchy novelty song to be used at a mail carrier function. Combining efforts, we put together a song called "Goin' Postal." It was an immediate hit with the carriers' membership. The organization purchased about 500 CD singles to be distributed with the convention welcome packages, which earned me a nice fee for producing and arranging the tune, and another fee for making the retail-ready CDs.

If you are doing business with karaoke companies, graphic illustrators, bridal shops/wedding planners, etc., try to address the local, regional, and national trade shows such organizations and industry professionals host. While exhibiting at these conventions may not be economical (or even feasible), you still might want to attend. They can be an excellent place to make regional/national contacts, and a good way to learn about any new developments in those industries. As an added benefit, you can write the trip off on your taxes (that fact alone makes it worthwhile to me!).

Commercials

Local businesses are an excellent source of commercial work. If you can convey creativity and energy in your commercials, potential clients will choose your packages, instead of having their local radio stations do it all. Auto dealerships, local fundraising events, festivals, and weekend entertainment hot spots represent the highest probability for commercial work.

Once you have demonstrated a proficiency in creating commercials, local broadcasters might even be open to the idea of paying you to do some of their spots for them. Remember that commercial creation is not necessarily their specialty, but stations will do it out of necessity to support their advertisers. Some stations use their own recording facility to pair pre-recorded material with voice-overs, while others seek out professional jingle houses for catchy little pieces, which they re-sell to advertisers who are without their own produced spots. A reliable, creative studio owner to whom they can outsource this work may be just what some of them are looking for. Whether you are creating the entire commercial from scratch, or simply creating the background music for someone else to add voice-overs, this is a customer source worth exploring.

Recorded Evidence

A market segment that has provided me with some of the most humorous, intriguing, and memorable work of my career has been that of police departments, attorneys, and private detectives. In even simple legal matters such as divorces and contract negotiations, recordings of phone conversations, face-to-face conversations, and other video/audio needs are a lot more effective and credible with slick studio processing.

Using your parametric EQ, noise reduction unit, and sonic enhancer effects, you can add clarity and detail to recordings that otherwise would not be viable as legal evidence. The significant thing about this work is that it's not time-intensive, but it can be profitable. You can make some bold commercial offerings. For example, you can boast, "If I cannot make this recording clearer and easy to understand, there will be no fee." In some cases, a lot is riding on this type of evidence. Trial attorneys will pay top dollar for your service if you are effective. And they say crime doesn't pay!

chapter **7**
The Demo

If there is one tool with which you have a chance to spread your feathers and strut your stuff, it's your studio demo. The demo allows you to differentiate yourself from the competition, and show your prospects that you are the real deal. A good demo is an impressive response to questions about the quality of your work. Without it, you will fumble through your collection of DATs, cassettes, and CDs, trying to find samples of your work to play for your prospects. You operate a recording studio, so it is unacceptable to be without a finely tuned, hard-hitting demo of your work.

A Smart Layout

The same guideline used for business cards, websites, and email applies to your demo: keep it simple. All forms of presentation work best when they're straightforward and easy to follow. A CD demo can cover a wide diversity of topics while allowing the listener to focus on what applies to his or her project. Modern software programs even allow the compilation of CD/DVD demos that can deliver both audio and visual images, but will still play as audio-only demos for regular CD players.

While there are no steadfast rules for making a studio demo, there are a few techniques that I learned the hard way, but which you can use to help maximize your impact on a demo:

- Begin your demo with a personal welcome and introduction. As a nice touch, use your own original music underneath. I recommend using up-tempo, positive music.

- Place as many examples of your work on the CD as you want, but don't duplicate genres. Unless, of course, you design the demo as a target for only one style of artist, show your range and diversity with examples of your rock, country, hip-hop, etc., recordings.

- Don't run all the music together as one performance. Include each style as its own separate, numbered track, which will give the listener the opportunity to select only cuts of interest. It will also allow you to direct prospects to those sections that make sense for their projects.

- Always get permission and/or mechanical licenses for the material you use in your demo. Again, the Harry Fox Agency is an excellent source for obtaining mechanical licensing for the previously recorded compositions of other artists. (See Chapter 5, "Music Licensing.")

- Close your demo with a pleasant message, and invite the listener to visit your facility. On my demos, I always tell the listeners that I am looking forward to working with them.

- Package your demo as professionally as you can afford to. There is nothing wrong with using PC-based software to create your own labels. These programs allow flexibility in changing demo contents, arrangements, and even your contact information or other studio particulars.

- Have your demo normalized and professionally mastered. A demo that presents selections of varying loudness, whether apparent or actual, will give the listener a poor impression of your abilities. If the listener's particular preference or style of music happens to be the one selection on your demo that sounds thin compared to the other tracks, your demo can cause you to lose work.

Sample Demo Layout

Here is the framework I used for my own demo, by track, which might also work for you: :

1. **A simple voice-over introduction using one of my original compositions as background.**
   You can consider this section to be a "welcome" to your studio.

2. **Pop sample:** I chose the song "Light in My Window" as the first example of my work because it's a clean, easy-to-listen-to recording. If my client base were comprised of alternative rocker types, I would have chosen to open the demo a lot more aggressively.

3. **R&B sample:** I used a song titled "Each Moment."

4. **Before-and-after sample:** This is a particularly effective tool in selling your production services to songwriters. First I included a noisy, poorly recorded version of what the songwriter had in mind for the song "Goin' Postal." Afterwards you hear the finished product, featuring a big-league vocalist, great players, and a solid recording.

5. **Hip-Hop sample:** Since today's hip-hop styles are so varied and ever changing, it might be a good idea to make a little vignette of several hip-hop songs to illustrate your flexibility. I used a song called "Love Muffin." For my purposes, this one example works.

6. **Christian sample:** This cut is actually a copy of a small promotional demo I did a few years ago to promote an "inspirational" compilation. The project, called "Music from Heaven," was designed to feature 12–15 selections on a single CD that served as a fundraiser for church participants. It was so popular it became a two-CD set. Keep in mind that, in addition to making a general demo of your work, you can create specialty demos to promote individual studio projects.

7. **"Nutty!":** There is no other way to describe it. This one might make one cringe, but I had my reasons for including it on this demo. When I first began my business, I would get work from artists who really were not what I would call polished, talented professionals. They included karaoke singers, amateur songwriters, or even aspiring artists with stars in their eyes. Sometimes these projects caused me to doubt the quality of my services—all I could think about was my competitors, whom I imagined were probably all working with great singers, musicians, and bands, and building a good, solid clientele while I was stuck with "nutty" work.

    As my business grew and I made increasingly more contacts, I discovered that these types of "nutty" projects are common to all studios at one time or another. The truth is that there is more bad talent than great talent in the world. When this kind of stuff does come your way, don't sweat it! As you build a reputation for yourself, strive for excellence in your work. The better talent will eventually hear about you and seek you out. Just remember that while you can't make a star out of everyone, you can give each client your best effort.

8. **Novelty songwriter sample:** This is another example of a before-and-after songwriter demo. Titled "You're So Lame," it's a joking nod to the NASCAR champion Jeff Gordon, and a parody of "You're So Vain" by Carly Simon. Although I was a big fan of Jeff's, the writer of this song was active in the "Fans Against Gordon Movement" that was popular at the time.

    You don't have to limit the before-and-after technique to songwriter demos. If your specialty is remixes, demonstrate your before-and-after remix qualities. Mastering examples work well, also.

9. **Jazz sample:** I included a nice example of a simple jazz trio who found great popularity in the Midwest.

10. **Epilogue:** This is the place to thank the listeners and invite them to visit your studio. Mention your location, phone number, and website. If you really want to close your demo with a bang, offer a freebie such as a recording tip sheet, a discount, or promotional items like hats, golf balls, or even guitar strings.

Other nifty ideas to include on demos:

- Before-and-after example of pitch correction technology illustrating your ability to correct even the most sour, off-pitch vocalist.
- A dramatic demonstration of what a great condenser mic can impart to an acoustic instrument.
- An educational message about reverb, compression, or noise gates.

With a little imagination, you can easily construct your demo to be a memorable selling tool.

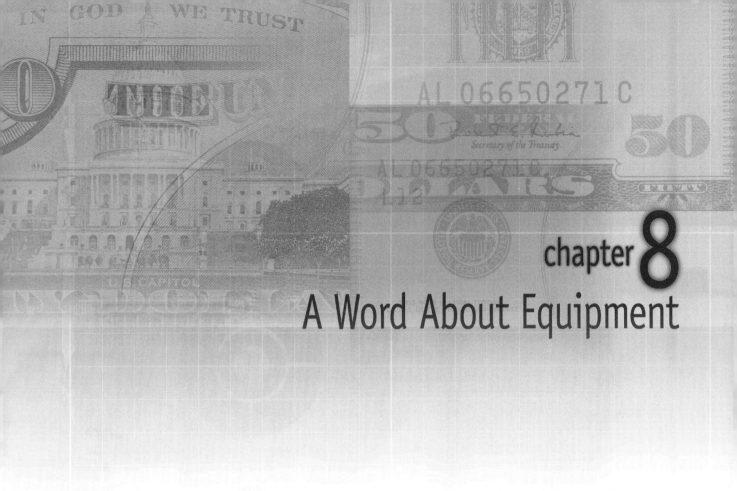

chapter 8
A Word About Equipment

When it comes to equipment selection, know your customer!

As you assemble and grow your studio, you must have a clear understanding of your market. Understanding your client base as it relates to your area of expertise will provide you with a solid foundation for making equipment (and other business) choices.

While it's challenging to make recommendations for equipment choices and a specific studio design without knowing you, your market, and your preferences, I recognize that your choices are vitally important to the success or failure of your business. Fortunately, there is an endless supply of readily available journals, instructional materials, and equipment retailers to help you with your studio design. Although I generally only make specific equipment recommendations in one-on-one, private, coaching-type situations, I do have some overall suggestions that I would like to share here.

 Essential Things to Consider

When thinking about new equipment, consider these questions:

- Will this equipment allow me to command a higher price, or help me bring in more business?
- Will this equipment make operating my studio easier?
- For the same price, what alternative options are available?
- Is there a used equipment alternative available?

The world of recording technology is scintillating and exciting, and the rapid pace of advancement in new technologies might make you feel you need to run out and purchase new equipment just to keep up. When you have had a little success, you will probably be temped to buy that first piece of high-end equipment that all the major players use. Before you spend, always ask yourself: "What do I really need?" Be wary of selling your talent short and over-spending in an attempt to add value and credibility to your business—a common trap for many studio owners.

I remember purchasing my first Neumann: a glorious U87. Up until that acquisition, my kingpin mic was an AT-4050—certainly no slouch, but it just didn't give me the self-assuredness about my sound that a Neumann would. For the longest time, obtaining a U87 was a part of my business plan.

I found out quickly that even though the U87 was a wonderful piece of equipment, I didn't have a customer base that appreciated or demanded it. Besides, in reality, the U87 really didn't sound measurably better than the 4050. A week after I bought the mic, it dawned on me that, for what I had spent, I could have bought another AT-4050, a back-up ART Pro MPA mic preamp, some new mic stands, extra cables, and another digital tuner for one of my booths—and still have had a couple hundred bucks left over!

Of course, I am not saying that you should avoid purchasing a Neumann U87 (which is a killer mic), but I am saying that purchasing the Neumann was not a good business decision for me at that point. To appease my own misguided sense of technical need, I made an emotional decision instead of a logical one. Had I been more rational and purchased all the equipment appropriate to my business and customer base, I would have increased my capabilities, added top-notch back-up equipment, and even minimized my set-up time between sessions.

Shiny new gadgets and gizmos are wonderful. One of the cool benefits of owning a studio is that we get to buy and play with new toys; but the caveat here is to avoid falling into the trap of buying toys that serve no purpose for growing your business. When you consider a new addition to your racks, put ego and love for technology aside, and consider only your studio needs.

Given the vast array of technology available to the modern recordist, it would be impossible to cover the topic adequately in one book, let alone in one chapter. However, over the years I have learned both tricks and pitfalls with regards to choosing equipment worth mentioning here. I hope my insights make you a better shopper.

Approaches to Equipment

There are three basic approaches in equipping your studio; and each presents benefits and limitations:

No. 1: Computer-Based Recording Systems

Computer-based systems, judged by sheer volume of sales, are the fastest growing recording systems in popularity. The allure of these systems is that they combine features like a mixer, multi-track recorder, sound effects processing, drum machines, and even synthesizer sounds, all into one simple-to-understand, easy-to-install package. Add to that the ability to turn one's home computer into a recording studio, and it is not hard to understand why these products are selling like hotcakes.

Unfortunately for the new recordist, computer-based systems also offer the greatest potential for disappointment. To the untrained eye, computer-recording suites appear to be the end-all solution to making great music. They are packaged smartly and are stocked with screen graphics that look just like the sophisticated multi-track units used by the pros. Sadly, the reality is that most of the cheesy computer/musical interfaces that come with many of these systems are not capable of delivering sound suitable for much more than tinkering around.

Most of these so-called "total recording" packages offer a severely limited number of analog inputs, which makes recording things like drums and multiple musical instruments impossible. I can't tell you how many studio owners I have encountered who were sure that their S/PDIF, MIDI, or other digital interfaces would be all they ever needed, but then realize too late that acoustic instruments and vocals will always be a vital component of modern music. A professional studio *must* be equipped to handle these needs.

Some of the better, moderately priced computer-recording interfaces do offer more analog inputs, but still fall horribly short of delivering capabilities that a professional can build a reputation on. Many of these packages have a computer interface card with a whole slew of XLR, RCA, and other connectors attached in a snake-type arrangement.

You will find that in the studio, the constant connecting, tugging, and disconnecting of mics, effects, and instruments takes a significant toll on equipment. It is hard enough to maintain the integrity of connections that are hard-wired to substantial, permanent wall panels and patch bays, without trying to manage manipulations with a rinky-dink $300 sound card connection.

When entering the world of computer-based recording, one caveat: beware of sound quality! It is just not reasonable to think that moderately priced computer-based, multi-track/interface packages are going to offer you A/D converters, effects, compressors, and mic options that deliver a truly professional-quality sound.

Manufacturers such as Avalon, Manley Labs, Focusrite, Neumann, AKG, and Audio Technica, to name a few, put a lot of research and development into their audio products. It is foolish to think that you can achieve the sound of the masters by using your computer and a cheap interface. Trust me, it ain't gonna happen! Don't misunderstand—I am a big fan of computer-based recording when it is approached sensibly. MOTU, for example, makes some of the most durable, formidable-sounding computer-based technology imaginable; and who can say anything negative about the wonderful Pro Tools computer-based recording suites?

If your modality choice is a computer-based system, here are some questions to consider:

- Will this system provide me enough quality inputs to handle every type of recording I wish to do?

- Is my computer powerful enough to provide the performance offered in the software package?

- How do the microphone preamps of my system compare to those of competitive mixing consoles and outboard gear?

- How compatible will this system be with other equipment?

- Is this equipment serviceable locally? Are replacement parts readily available?

- What are the expandable capabilities of this system (important as you grow and need more inputs, effects, and mixing capabilities)?

Applied properly, computer-based recording systems can serve as the hub around which a successful studio can be built. Just be careful when entering this arena. A good rule of thumb when purchasing a computer-based recording system is to compare both the features and price of any system with that of an alternative technology. The chances are good that a computer system, which sells for a fraction of the cost of other recording technologies, will likewise offer only a fraction of the performance features, too.

If you do decide to purchase one of these systems, it is essential to obtain it from a reputable, local retailer who also has expertise in conventional methods of recording, and who can demonstrate to you first-hand the various features, benefits, and shortcomings of the gear you are considering.

No. 2: Digital Audio Work Stations (DAWS)

From the early days of the workhorse Roland VS-1680 recorder, to the powerhouse packages offered today, DAWS technology has progressed by leaps and bounds. Designed to be one-stop shopping experiences for those wanting to set up personal studios, single-purchase DAWS have spawned many commercial studio ventures.

Modern DAWS offer as many as twenty-four tracks, and features like onboard effects, phantom power, XLR mic inputs, built-in CD burners, mastering software, and beat boxes. The newest machines also offer a variety of interface options for hooking up to computer-based systems.

For the new studio owner, DAWS offer several advantages over computer-based systems. First, DAWS are a substantial piece of equipment more suitable for the rigors of frequent mic and equipment connections. By offering actual faders, mixing and tweaking are easier and more efficient. A physical mixing console enables a client to manipulate a fader to show you what he or she had in mind.

As in the case with computer-based systems, the onboard compressors, mic preamps, and processors are not going to be competitive with those on traditional outboard units. In my opinion, except for the ultra high-end computer-based systems, DAWS are much more compatible with outboard gear, and are better at allowing you to realize the benefits that equipment like a tube mic preamp can deliver.

DAWS usually offer 2–4 analog XLR mic inputs, with another 4–6 being 1/4-inch balanced TRS. This is certainly an advantage over most consumer-level computer-based systems, but still short of a traditional mixing console's twenty-four or more XLR inputs. Nonetheless, DAWS do offer enough access to do traditional recording with both electronic and real instruments.

One of the disadvantages of many DAWS is the size of their view screens. Many of the entry-level units offer a small screen that may be hard to read and interpret during busy sessions. If you can afford it, select a unit that has either a large screen, or even better, two screens (one for track monitoring and one for recorder function monitoring). Still better, seek out a unit that offers the ability to connect to a remote monitor.

No. 3: Modular (Traditional) Recording

By "modular," I am referring to a traditional mixing board for inputs and outputs, and a stand-alone recording unit to capture your creations. Twenty years ago, this type of recording was the only thing available. Back then; it was difficult for the average working stiff to enter the business. Somewhere in the '70s, however, companies such as Fostex and TASCAM started aggressively offering more modestly priced 8-, 16-, and 24-track tape recorders in an effort to capture this new and unexploited market. Today, there are countless separate equipment selections—options for digital boards, analog boards, hybrid boards, and even boards designed to interface with computer-based systems.

As far as recording modalities go, we can choose from analog tape, digital tape, and a whole slew of proprietary digital recording formats, with more coming up everyday. Otari, TASCAM, Alesis, and Mackie are only a few of the many companies offering digital hard drive, stand-alone recorders.

By far, the most popular recording modality of all, the Alesis ADAT is still a formidable force with first-time studio owners. The worldwide use of ADAT makes it the most sensible choice for studio owners wanting to be compatible with other studios. The ADAT is so much a staple of modern recording technology that even high-end, Grammy-caliber studios usually have them onboard.

While many of the new computer programs and DAWS offer many bells and whistles, none of them have the portability, popularity, and compatibility that ADAT does. The newer systems are growing more popular every year, but the ADAT format remains an affordable alternative for those recordists wanting a higher level of flexibility than that offered by the typical studio-in-a-box systems.

For true professional sound quality and features, modular recorders are still without peer. By allowing the engineer to employ things like discreet, class-A mic preamps, compressors, and effects, this type of setup will deliver the best recordings.

Do not fret though; use of the proper outboard gear, when combined with a DAWS or good computer-based system can rival the big boys—enough so that 99% of listeners will not be able to tell the difference. Fortunately, though, no equipment in the world will replace attentive mixing, solid engineering, and creative production.

Hot Equipment Tips

1. Monitors

Perhaps the most important studio investment you will ever make is in near field monitors. If you plan to do mixing, choosing the proper monitor can make the difference between the success and failure of your business. Monitors are *that* important.

This may unnerve some equipment manufacturers and so-called studio experts, but it is advice from someone who depends on his studio to pay the mortgage and put food on the table: Forget all the horse-manure technical discussions about which monitor is very flat or completely accurate. A monitor must offer you only one thing—the ability to make a mix that will sound good no mater what you play it back on. A monitor may sound like crap to everyone else in the world, but if you can mix on it and consistently have your customers smile, then you have a great monitor. Not all humans hear the same way; so logically, there can be no "best" monitor for everyone.

A couple important guidelines that will help you choose a great monitor:

- If you can afford only one set of monitors, purchase ones that offer 8-inch drivers.
- If you can afford them, purchase self-powered, bi-amped monitors.

Also, if you mix on tiny 5–6-inch monitors, you will have a natural tendency to mix in too much bass in order to achieve the type of playback sounds that are typical of today's music. The mix will sound great in the studio, but when your client takes the finished product home, it will sound muddy and too bassy on his or her own stereo.

In addition, small monitors do not provide the sonic clarity and tonal separation required for serious mixing. Despite the claims of manufacturers about the supposedly "rich" bass frequencies produced by their compact monitors, none of the moderately priced 5–6-inch monitors will deliver mixes that you can build a reputation on. Fortunately, there are some great, modestly priced, self-powered 8-inch monitors readily available. My favorites are:

- Event 20/20 BAS
- Mackie HR824
- Yamaha MSP10
- Event PS8
- M Audio BX8

We have all heard the story about the producer who mixed Grammy Award-winning songs on Yamaha NS10s. No disrespect to that producer, but these monitors don't work for me, and won't likely work for you, either. Powered eights sound better—much better! They also make mixing easier and listening less fatiguing.

To make the most accurate comparison possible, always choose monitors in an environment that allows you to make an A/B test with some other models. If there is a lot of noise from people testing guitars and amps at the retail outlet, simply ask a manager if they can open a bit early or stay a bit late to help you select the proper monitors in a quiet environment. As long as you actually intend to purchase monitors, most retailers will be cooperative in helping you.

On a final note, 5-inch monitors can be the kiss of death to your mixes, just as using a sub-woofer or too large of a driver can also ruin your mixes. In this case, too much monitor bass response will cause you to add too little bass in your mixes, leaving them thin and lifeless on the listener's own equipment.

2. Signal Path Processors and Equipment

Many of the world's most famous recordings are earmarked by a signature vocal sound that seems to hypnotize and captivate us no matter how many times we listen. A great vocalist is a good starting point. Almost as important, however, are the signal path and microphone in determining just how great the vocals sound in the final recording.

Beginning recordists first realize the shortcomings of their new equipment when they attempt to capture a great vocal performance. Then they realize that, as wonderful as the new DAWS and computer-based recording systems are, the inexpensive preamps and compressors found onboard these units just don't measure up to the specs offered by modern outboard gear.

Don't go out and spend $4,000 for a high-end mic preamp or compressor to record great vocals. Vocal processing equipment has benefited from the new technologies in the same way that recording systems have hit new highs. The following, sensibly priced units are some of my favorites:

- **Art Pro MPA**—two-channel tube mic preamp
- **Art Pro VLA**—two-channel tube compressor
- **Drawmer MX60 Front End One**—total one-channel vocal processor
- **Focusrite MH401 Tone Factory**—one-channel processor for guitar/vocals
- **Symetrix 528E Voice Processor**—yet another one-channel wonder
- **Focusrite MH400 VoiceMaster**—mic preamp, compressor, de-esser, EQ
- **Art Pro Channel**—another great one-channel total voice processor
- **Radius30 HHB Tube Compressor**—rivals high-end tube compressors
- **Fatman HHB Tube Compressor**—two-channel tube compressor
- **Behringer T1952 Tube Composer**—two-channel compressor, limiter, gate, and more
- **Behringer T1953 Tube Ultragain**—two-channel tube mic preamp

3. Microphones and Mic Simulators

Since I have gone out on a limb here in listing my favorite monitors and signal path equipment, I should say a little bit about microphones. Microphones are the first piece of equipment in line when recording voices or acoustic instruments, so it makes sense that choosing the proper mic can make or break your recordings. Make no mistake about it, for capturing live sounds, *nothing* can rival a high-quality condenser mic. Condensers offer signal sensitivity not achievable with the common, conventional dynamic mics used in live performances. At the absolute minimum, a studio must have two condenser mics on hand—a large diaphragm for vocals and ambient work, and a small diaphragm for acoustic instruments.

One of the more annoying and misleading trends in recording technology lately has been the mic simulator technology offered by various manufacturers. Some manufacturers include a feature that will supposedly allow your Shure SM58 to sound like a high-quality condenser mic, such as the AKG 414. While these devices can improve the quality of sounds recorded with an improper mic, nothing of this earth will make an SM58 sound like a Neumann.

It's easy for a recordist on a tight budget to buy into a sales pitch about what a new recorder will do. However, I have repeatedly seen the disappointment that these mic simulators have caused new studio owners who realize, three months down the road, that they are not capturing the same lush vocals that the studio owner down the street is able to get. Fortunately, modern manufacturing technologies have made great microphones affordable to studio owners on even the tightest of budgets.

Here is a list of what I consider to be the most affordable and effective microphones on the market:

- **AKG C3000**—this was the first consumer-level large diaphragm condenser mic offered to the general buying public. It remains one of the quietest, richest, and most dependable mics available at a budget price. Great vocal mic.

- **AKG C1000**—a small diaphragm condenser that works great on acoustic guitars, and can double for background vocals.

- **Audio Technica 4050**—this mic is a bit pricier, but at less than half the cost of a low-end Neumann, it is a tremendous value and is absolutely heavenly on vocals. (The economical 4040 model is likewise a great value.)

- **Rode NT1 and NT2**—two low-cost condenser vocal mics that offer unbelievable warmth and quality for the money.

- **Shure SM58**—perhaps the greatest and most famous of all dynamic mics of all time. An absolute workhorse as a drum and percussion mic.

- **Sennheiser 421**—this mic has been used successfully on everything from vocals to drums to bagpipes. A very versatile "third" mic choice. Works very well as an overhead mic on drum recordings.

- **Shure SM94**—a very articulate and precise mic for acoustic guitars.

- **Electro-Voice N/D 868**—a very efficient mic for capturing thunderous kick drum sounds.

- **Shure PG81**—a super low-cost small diaphragm condenser.

Unbelievably, the manner in which you purchase equipment has a great bearing on the manner in which equipment is offered to you in the future. Recently, we have all been bombarded by a plethora of new and exciting online and mail-order offers from vendors touting low prices and "front-door" delivery. The traditional neighborhood music store is no longer the only source for music-related gear. The competition for your business grows fiercer daily.

At the risk of ruffling even more feathers, I will say that I think mail order companies are wonderful, and I have used them myself a time or two. However, on larger purchases, I prefer using a dealer who services the products and offers hands-on demonstrations. (A word of caution: your local music retailer can be an important business partner now and in the future, so don't exploit his or her time by learning about equipment in-store, and then buying online. Recognize the value that actually trying the product out in person offers you!

4. Miscellaneous Items:

Some other things that no studio should be without:

- **Emergency power supply**—you can find these little devices in your local computer or gadget store. Since today's computer and DAWS systems do not consume a lot of power, it is relatively inexpensive to purchase an emergency power supply unit capable of keeping your equipment functioning in the event of a power failure. Saving just one vocal take during an outage will pay for your investment in such a system. Preventing the loss of an entire CD's worth of material is an even better reason for having a power backup supply in place all the time. To choose the proper unit, simply add up all the power consumption ratings of your equipment (in milli-amperes) and buy a unit capable of delivering this current for 10–15 minutes. A $150 investment can save your reputation.

- **Markertek foam**—this company sells excellent, economically priced sound insulation foam that come in 54- by 54-inch panels. This stuff works wonders, is available in a couple of different colors and thicknesses, and costs a minor fraction of what the name brand foam does. This stuff is terrific!

- **Digital Multimeter**—these units are available for as little as $20 from general hardware vendors like Home Depot or electronics outlets like Radio Shack, and can be absolute lifesavers in the studio. A DVM allows you to do things like test the continuity of a cable or connection, measure the voltage coming out of an outlet or battery, and even test the output of your outboard gear. You don't have to be an electrical engineer to use one, and having a DVM on hand will make keeping your studio operational a lot easier.

- **Drum jellies**—marketed under a variety of product names, these things are small, amber-colored "jellies" about the size of a silver dollar. Placed on a snare drum or tom-tom, they have the uncanny ability to remove that annoying, sustaining drum ring that can make great drum recordings impossible. Forget the duct tape, the trial-and-error noise gate experiments, and the homemade dampening concoctions. Go to your local drum store and pick up some of these goofy, but invaluable, things. The distinct drum recordings these lil' buggers produce will amaze you.

- **Amplifier baffles**—an amplifier baffle is nothing more than a homemade, wooden (usually hardwoods such as maple, poplar, oak, or ash) box filled with sound insulation. The baffle is used to cover a guitar amplifier after it's miked and ready to record. Baffles operate like mini sound booths, confining the sound to the "booth," and thereby allowing other instruments to be recorded at the same time. The baffle should be large enough to cover the amp and/or mic, and allow about two feet of clearance space (including the mic and stand) around each side, front and back. For the best tone, air needs to be able to move in and out of the enclosure easily, so a foam-covered 3-inch circular opening is usually a good idea. An amplifier baffle works well for that occasional guitarist who insists that his or her amp be cranked to "10" in order for him or her to achieve a desired tone.

Let me leave you with this analogy on equipment: When you build a house, your money should be put into the kitchen, bathrooms, windows, and doors. In the studio, the fundamentals are monitors, signal path processors, and mics. Choose well in these areas and you will have a great foundation on which to build sizzle!

chapter **9**
Studio Profiles

Studios are amazingly diverse. Depending on the skills, budget, and tastes of its owner, a studio can be designed to specialize in tracking, mixing, mastering, MIDI production, orchestral recordings, commercials, film scoring, and even sound effects for electronic games. This chapter takes a closer look at four uniquely different studios, and gives some insight into how and why they were built.

A Tuneman Productions

(Formerly Tommy's Tunes Productions)
Tom Volinchak, Owner
4707 New Road
Youngstown, OH 44515
(330) 792-5730
www.tunemanproductions.com

Like many of you, owning a studio was a lifelong dream for me. My first studio was a bedroom-based Fostex four-track unit that I built to pitch my own demos. After getting involved with the Nashville Songwriters Association, I recognized my need for more elaborate demos; so I upgraded to a Yamaha MT-8X eight-track cassette unit. Soon, other writers were hiring me to produce and record their demos, and before I knew it, a gospel group employed my services to produce a full-blown CD. As more and more people demonstrated their willingness to pay for my services, I gained confidence; and in 1995, I took the leap and made recording my full-time career.

I am fortunate to have played with most of the area's best musicians. I have a long list of musical contacts made through years of playing, teaching, and my work with the Nashville Songwriter's Association. I also nurture and maintain good relationships with the salespeople at all the local music stores.

Based on my contacts, I am able to gather a lot of information about who the hot area bands are, where they're recording, how much they're paying, and what the local buzz is about my competition. These same contacts also allow me to spread the word about my studio.

Studio competition for band business is terribly fierce. The abundance of studios and the limited amount of bands seeking to record fueled an uprising of studios in this area willing to provide service in $25-per-hour range. Since there is no future in booking this kind of business, I have directed my focus toward educating my prospects and selling value-added services to command a fair price for my work.

The products that provide me the highest profits are songwriter demos, and projects by individual singers and rap/hip-hop artists. Having a nice catalog of original music and being able to play multiple instruments gives me an edge over competitors who generally have to hire more musicians to get similar results. When I do have to hire players, I am always able to get my area's most capable talent.

Other specialties that provide steady income and profit to me are ethnic genres such as Polish, Slovenian, Irish, Greek, and Mexican. My reputation as an accomplished accordion player has earned me confidence and trust with these types of clients as well. Additionally, I've developed the niche market of recording books-on-tape projects. I also exploit the portability of my gear to land the occasional mobile recording.

I don't enjoy computer-based recording, so I don't fool around with it. For me, there is simply no joy in schlepping MIDI devices, time-code puzzles, and complex digital/analog morphing. Likewise, I have absolutely no interest in film scoring, video synchronizing, or Surround Sound wizardry. However, the popularity of my studio does generate calls for this stuff, so when such clients come in, I refer them to competent studios that specialize in those areas. In return for my time and trouble, I always get a nice little finder's fee.

Once I realized my strengths, weaknesses, and desires, I put together a studio wish list that looked like this:

- A hard disk medium for my primary recording (the benefits: no rewind time, digital editing, and great sound quality)
- 16–24 tracks of ADATS (I needed to be compatible with other studios.)
- Enough physical space to comfortably record a five-piece band
- The flexibility to do mobile recordings (in order to go after the church and concert recordings nobody else was pursuing)
- Adequate storage for multiple projects

I built this studio in my home, and allocated for it a 30' × 40' area. Fortunately, I am located on a quiet, dead-end street. and have plenty of room for parking. I opted for an 18' × 16' main booth, two 8' × 8' vocal/utility booths, and a 16' × 18' control room, with the remaining space used for storage and a lounging area.

For equipment, I decided on two Roland VS1680s and three Syquest Syjet removable 1.5-gigabyte hard drive storage devices. I chose the VS1680 for the multiple features it offers for the buck. While this unit is not necessarily designed for commercial studio work, with its adequate backup (I later purchased a third unit), data storage, and outboard gear, the recorder serves me very well.

All my outboard gear is mounted in portable racks to afford the flexibility of doing mobile recordings and off-site mixing. The following is a total equipment list:

- Three Roland VS1680 recording units, each with two effects cards
- Three ADAT XT 8-track recorders
- Three Syquest Syjet drives with thirty 1.5-gig cartridges
- Two Art Pro MPA tube mic preamps
- Two Art Pro VLA tube compressors
- Aphex 107 2-channel tube mic preamp
- TASCAM 202 MkII cassette deck
- TASCAM DA30 MkII DAT recorder
- Computer-based CD burner
- Lexicon PCM-80 effects processor
- Lexicon MPX-1 effects processor
- Art FX effects processor
- Four dbx 163 compressors
- Behringer Ultra Curve EQ unit
- Two Aphex 104 4-channel compressors
- Two Aphex 105 4-channel noise gates
- Hush noise reduction unit
- BBE 462 Sonic Maximizer
- Neumann U87 condenser mic
- AT4050 condenser mic
- Equitek E-300 condenser mic
- AKG C3000 condenser mic
- Two Shure SM 84 condenser mics
- Two AKG C-1000 condenser mics
- Four Shure SM58 mics
- Four Shure SM57 mics
- One pair of Tannoy PBM-6.5 monitors
- One pair of Event Bas 20/20 monitors
- One pair of custom-built monitors with 12-inch JBL drivers
- EuroDesk 8-bus analog mixer

I operate the studio as a smoke-free environment, and when not booked with recording sessions, I always try to keep things buzzing by offering training classes, guest seminars, or even community service work opportunities.

I believe that one critical thing has contributed to my success and made my experience as a studio owner pleasurable: my commitment to work only on those projects that match my capabilities. I take pride in doing what is best for the client, even if it means referring him or her to a more compatible studio.

 **Big Red Studios**

Rick Dixon, Owner
1019 Sixteenth Avenue South
Nashville, TN 37203
(615) 867-6421

Right in the heart of Nashville's historic Music Row on Sixteenth Avenue, tucked neatly away in a converted attic, is one of the city's best song demo factories, Big Red Studios. Owner Rick Dixon has produced tracks for writers like Richard Addrissi ("Never My Love"), Casey Kelly Kostas ("Soon"), and Robert Jason ("Ain't Your Ordinary Girl"). Rick has developed a solid reputation for getting a demo done right the first time at a very economical price.

Music Row is unlike anywhere else in the world; the abundance of recording studios there has driven prices down to painfully low levels. While this has been good for the multitude of songwriters who do business in Nashville, it has played absolute havoc with those trying to make a living in the studio trade. Both the rates of new studio openings and existing studio closings are nothing less than mind-boggling.

To the observer, Rick's success centers on several strengths that he has identified and focused on. The man is an accomplished singer/songwriter/guitar player who still works vigorously on his own original material. Since moving to Nashville, he has also taught himself to play drums, bass, and keyboards, while constantly striving to improve his recording skills. These multiple talents enable Rick to provide many songwriters with an economical demo on which he can totally produce, perform, and record the various parts. His advantage is that most competing studios have to hire outside musicians at considerable costs to get the same results as Rick's one-man-band productions. Rick is able to offer his clients a very competitive price that provides him with a good profit margin.

Rick has not only established strong working relationships with many of Nashville's so-called "A-team" players for more elaborate projects, but he has also hooked up with up-and-coming Nashville producer Garret Parris—who compliments Rick's talents perfectly. On detailed projects, Rick's quality competes with the major studios, and he does so at a price that attracts new artists like bees to honey.

Another one of Rick's strengths is his ability to comprehend what the songwriter has in mind for a song, then to translate that quickly and economically to the session players he works with. The result is a demo that usually far exceeds the expectations of the client.

The most impressive part of his operation is that, unlike studios that cut their own profits in order to get business, Rick has found a way to offer reasonable prices while maintaining a solid profit margin—he reduces his production costs. I can think of no better example to illustrate the benefits of focusing in on one's strengths.

Rick's equipment includes a Ramsa DA7 board, ADATS, and a Fostex D-90 or Digital Performer for tracking. His preamps and compressors include an Art Pro MPA, Aphex, and Presonus. The studio also features both digital and acoustic drums all set up and ready to go, and an Alesis QS8 as a staple synth. There are also 1965 Fender Deluxe and Polytone Mega Brute guitar amps, which are hardwired into the main mixing console to allow for fast setups. His monitors are the Event BAS 20/20 Actives and Yamaha NS-10s.

At the time of this writing, Rick was in the process of creating a website for his studio.

Karma Recording Studio

Michael and Sally Rich, Owners
337 West 6th Street
San Pedro, CA 90731
(310) 856-7444
www.karmastudio.com

It bears mentioning: success is a process, not an event. If there ever was a living, breathing example of this principle, it is the Richs' experiences with Karma. Like many of us, Michael and Sally got started in the business when he was playing for peanuts in local bands, looking for ways to increase his income, and staying close to the music that he loved. For him, recording friends and local bands in a self-built, home studio was the perfect solution.

Eventually, Michael built a reputation for his work. While striving to improve his recordings, he decided to obtain some formal training to augment his seat-of-the-pants experience. So in 1995, he enrolled in the recording program at The Los Angeles Recording Institute of Technology.

After completing six months of study, Michael capitalized on an opportunity to work at the world-renowned Record Plant in the Los Angeles area. His experiences there included working with multiple SSL consoles and 5.1 Surround Sound, and invaluable exposure to Record Plant artists Celine Dion, Babyface, Bob Dylan, and Toni Braxton.

Desiring more autonomy in his work, he left the Record Plant, and went on to do some freelance work at other L.A. studios such as Enterprise and Small World Studios in Venice, California. While freelancing, Michael met his future wife, who began working with him. The two of them envisioned their own professional-quality studio.

In 2000, the Richs put a business plan together, accumulated equipment along the way, secured a $160,000 loan from a local investor, and built their 2000-square-foot, state-of-the-art Karma Studios. Michael was able to buy the investor out only two short years after building the studio. Now that's what I call building success!

Karma is built around Pro Tools 5.2, using the Mackie Digital 8-bus console. A full equipment list is available on their website for the curious. For compatibility, the studio does offer 20-bit Alesis ADAT technology.

During our interview, Michael talked very passionately about the features of Karma that fill him with pride. His focus is less on the equipment than what he calls "catering to creativity." This studio owner has found that his personal path to success centers on taking the time to personalize each project. Michael likes to sit down with his clients beforehand and actually map out what they want to accomplish. Then he's equipped to present them with a realistic budget for required hours.

In his experience, Michael says that musicians really don't know how many hours a project is going to take, and in general, place their confidence in him once he explains the various factors that will come into play during their sessions. He finds that his clients usually spend a bit more than they had originally budgeted, but in the end, feel that they received value from dealing with someone who took the time to gain insight into their music.

SALES TIP! *As a way to generate new business, Michael regularly makes free studio time available to both up-and-coming bands and established bands that have never recorded before. He schedules the free recordings to take place during his downtime between regular sessions. By giving away a free song to bands, Michael drums up new prospects, as these initially freebie clients often return to do demos or full CDs. A terrific promotional tool that generates a lot of pass-along among musicians, this offer is an excellent way for Michael to keep the Karma name fresh and alive in the local music scene. Offering a free session also presents a great opportunity to try out a new piece of equipment or new techniques.*

Michael's talents and credentials prove themselves not only in his accomplishments, but also in his well-defined business plan that includes his efforts to add value to his services. He has truly mastered the art of commanding a price commensurate with his experience. For him, operating a studio is a labor of love, which means that the desire to achieve excellence is never compromised. Visit his website. As you read about his career path, remember that he did it all on his own.

A Sharp Recording Studio

Jeff Cripps, Owner
339 Belmore Road
Riverwood, NSW 2210
(Sidney, Australia)
011-612-9153-9988
www.asharp.com.au

Jeff Cripps and the A Sharp studio deserve mention for their unique slant on recording. Jeff is the owner, but he has a business arrangement with two other producer/engineers who bring both their own equipment and recording chops to the A Sharp package. By combining resources, Jeff is able to offer analog tape recording, digital tape recording, and hard drive-based recording and editing.

From a technological standpoint, the diversity of its recording formats allows A Sharp to attract artists within a wide range of styles without compromising a thing. By having professional partnerships within the studio, Jeff is also able to draw from a large pool of talent for his sessions, and seldom has to hire outside musicians or technicians to get the job done. The partnership approach also has minimized the costs that all three participants would have had to pay if they started their own individual studios.

Like many, Jeff began his recording career in his home on a cassette-based four-track unit. He progressed to an eight-track, and eventually decided to attend a local TV production and sound school. There Jeff found that what he had already learned by trial-and-error was in fact, based on sound recording principles. The fortification and polish he received in school gave him a little more confidence to go into business for himself.

The A Sharp website is chock-full of great pictures, an impressive client list, and a few helpful stories to help educate folks on the right way to make a recording. (This is a great way to bring people to your site—you might want to consider posting a "free recording tips" section on your own!)

Jeff also proudly and openly advertises his rates on the website. (As discussed earlier, this can be a tricky sales technique because it sets you up for comparison. I urge you to talk price only after the prospect has fallen completely in love with your studio. Once a business has achieved a certain level of success and reputation, price is a much less sensitive issue; customers feel it is a privilege and an accomplishment to record with that studio, and upfront pricing is easier to work with.)

Jeff reports finding the same downward pricing pressure Down Under that we battle here in the States. He combats the bargain-basement attack by selling those features that his competitors cannot offer. In addition to offering professional recording formats, A Sharp features a large, live room that can generate tones not available in smaller, makeshift home studios. Jeff also offers his prospects recorded samples illustrating what guitars, horns, and drums can sound like when captured in the proper environment.

In many cases, Jeff has been able to win business away from much larger studios by offering suitable technology and great ambience for an economical package price. He usually refers the less professional, smaller-budget prospects to the studios better suited to perform that work, and chooses to stay focused on finding clients who need exactly what he has to offer.

The old saying that "no man is an island" is especially applicable to studio owners. Having fingertip access to service partners who can offer support quickly and efficiently is an absolute lifesaver. I am always searching for new companies to support my studio efforts, and I encourage you to do the same. The following resources have demonstrated superior service and impeccable reputations:

A Educational Resources

Education is an important part of owning a studio, and fortunately, sources are varied. Seat-of-the-pants experience, apprenticeships, formal recording schools, magazines, books and journals, and even correspondence courses are available to help keep us knowledgeable. There isn't a standard, accepted method of getting an education in studio ownership, but there is one very good rule of thumb: no matter how much we know, or think we know, we always need to expand our horizons. The technological pace at which the recording industry is moving is nothing less than astounding; and if we don't keep up, it will pass us by.

1. Schools

While representing only a sampling of schools available, I know these to be significant:

Full Sail, Real World Education
330 University Boulevard
Winterpark, FL 37792
(800) 226-7625
www.fullsail.com

The Full Sail School is bursting with great equipment, like SSL and Neve consoles, and has well-equipped studio workstations for the students. They offer a thorough classroom education that even covers the economic/business aspects of the entertainment industry. Degrees in audio engineering, film production, sound for digital animation, and sound for films are available. The list of guest speakers and workshop leaders reads like a who's who of the music industry. If you are thinking about a full-blown audio education, this is a great school to consider.

SAE Institute
269 W. 40th Street
New York, NY 10018
(212) 944-9123
www.sae.edu

SAE has schools in New York, Nashville, Miami, and other locations all over the world. These schools are terrific, offering a wide diversity of programs. Some of the degrees are coordinated and validated by nearby universities or colleges. SAE trains students on the latest technology, and features a revolving door of well-credentialed, nationally known guest speakers and trainers. This is one of the finest private schools in the country.

L.A. Recording Workshop
5278 Lanershim Blvd.
North Hollywood, CA 91601
(818) 763-7400
www.recordingcareer.com

The L.A. Recording Workshop is a powerhouse school, offering instruction on fourteen different consoles. Their equipment list includes such industry standards as SSL, Otari, Studer, and Pro Tools. There are multiple programs available, as well as career guidance services.

The Recording Workshop
455 Massieville Road
Chillicothe, OH 45601
(800) 848-9900
www.recordingworkshop.com

The recording workshop in central Ohio offers eight studios and a variety of programs that stress real-life work situations, and focuses on building their graduates' careers. The program offers a very impressive and comprehensive Pro Tools curriculum. The school is closely associated with Capital University and offers credits toward that university's Bachelor of Science degree.

The Conservatory of Recording Arts and Sciences
2300 East Broadway Road
Tempe, AZ 85282
(800) 562-6383
www.audiorecordingschool.com

The Conservatory is a good sound school featuring a recording education designed to place students into industry jobs. They offer multiple training studios equipped with SSL and Neotek consoles, and very well-appointed mixing stations. They were the first authorized Pro Tools educator.

Career Connection, Inc.

(800) 295-4433

www.radioconnection.com

This unique company offers on-the-job training programs in conjunction with participating recording studios and radio and TV stations. For the individual who wants to learn recording technology while holding down a full-time job, this company presents some interesting options.

2. Home Study

Golden Ears Audio Training

13351-D

Riverside Drive

Sherman Oaks, CA 91423

(800) 600-1543

www.kiqproductions.com

The Golden Ears home-study program consists of eight CDs designed to bring your skills to a new level. The course covers EQ, effects, stereo anomalies, and a variety of crucial sequences designed to help the student make better recordings. While this is not a school, it is one of the best educational tools available to the studio owner.

The Audio Institute of America (AIA)

814 46th Avenue

San Francisco, CA 94121

(415) 752-0701

audioinst@earthlink.net

www.audioinstitute.com

AIA is perhaps the most complete home-study/correspondence course for the aspiring audio engineer/studio owner. One of the most impressive features of this program is not only the technical education provided, but also the insight provided with regards to building your own studio, finding a recording industry job, and even operating a successful business. An equally attractive feature of this program is that the student does not need to possess a large amount of equipment to master the material presented. This course garners the highest accolades and world acclaim. Check it out!

Find a complete listing of recording schools here: http://www.modrec.com/schools/index.php

Please note that in addition to the educational resources listed, many colleges and universities throughout the nation offer fully degreed programs in a wide array of music business disciplines— including recording. I urge you to look into them.

3. Essential Periodicals

MIX
6400 Hollis Street
Suite 12
Emeryville, CA 94608
www.mixonline.com

Mix is a magazine designed for recording industry professionals who demand the most current information available. Much of the equipment featured is out of the budget range of most individual studio owners, but for those who dream of Grammys, gold records, and major movie scores, this magazine is a staple.

Recording
5412 Idylwild Trail
Suite 100
Boulder, CO 80301-3523
(800) 582-8326
www.recordingmag.com

Recording is a delightful magazine that hits home with studio owners of all sizes. It features product tests, studio profiles, industry events, and recording techniques. One of the cool products they offer is a series of CDs entitled *Playback*, which is comprised of a substantial library of loops, techniques, and practical tips provided by industry professionals. It even includes reader tapes for learning critique. *Recording* is an excellent companion, especially for those who don't live in or near major music markets, but thirst for mainstream information.

Home Recording Magazine
6 East 32nd Street
11th Floor
New York, NY 10016
(800) 937-0420
www.homerecordingmag.com

Home Recording is a clear, concise, easy-to-understand collection of product reviews, studio profiles, recording techniques, and interviews with successful studio owners. The magazine focuses on topics that relate well to the average studio owner, and there is a very friendly feel to the magazine. Of particular note are the regular columns that describe techniques that can make day-to-day life in the studio a lot easier.

Electronic Musician
9800 Metcalf
Overland Park, KS 66212
(800) 245-2737
www.emusic.com

Electronic Musician covers a variety of electronic technologies closely related to the recording industry. New software, synthesizers, sound modules, artist profiles, and industry trends are all thoroughly addressed. This magazine serves as a nice compliment to the mainstream recording magazines.

EQ Magazine
PO Box 0532
Baldwin, NY 11510
(212) 378-0449
www.eqmag.com

EQ is a cutting-edge periodical geared toward the business side of our industry. As with most recording magazines, EQ covers new equipment, recording techniques, and key interviews. It's not always easy to find on the shelves, but well worth the search.

4. Books and Publications—Technology and Industry-Specific

The Recording Industry Sourcebook
Artistpro Publishing

The Sourcebook is *the* definitive source for everything you want to know about the recording industry. This annual lists studios, equipment manufacturers, producers, record execs, management companies, etc. It's particularly useful to those studio owners involved in getting their clients' music heard and sold.

Producing in the Home Studio with Pro Tools
By David Franz
Berklee Press Publications, 2001

Even if you are not a Pro Tools user, it helps to be knowledgeable about this popular line of recording suites. This book supplies how-tos of all their equipment, along with some very helpful tips on operating a studio.

How to Build a Small Budget Recording Studio from Scratch: With 12 Tested Designs
By Mike Shea and F. Alton Everest
McGraw/Hill/TAB Electronics, 2002

Everest is an accomplished acoustical engineer with an impressive curriculum vitae. His book is filled with excellent technical tips and money saving ideas to help you construct your studio.

The Songwriter's Market
Writers Digest Books

Updated and reissued annually, this book focuses on helping songwriters get their songs to market. It's a valuable tool to the studio owner because it lists many sources for new material, reveals the record labels that will accept outside material, and lists the songwriter organizations that support both new and experienced writers. This book also provides many sources of potential income and extra services that you can provide to your clients.

5. Books and Publications—Career and Business

Life Is a Contact Sport: Ten Great Career Strategies That Work
By Kenneth Kragen, Jefferson Graham, and Ken Kragen
Quill, 1996

For years, this book has served as a staple for sales professionals and business owners. This book illustrates how, using basic communications skills, you can vastly increase the number of people who know you. I strongly recommend it.

How to Gain an Extra Hour Every Day: More Than 500 Time-Saving Tips
By Ray Josephs
Plume, 1992

This book offers many useable examples of how to maximize your day and gain efficiency in daily activities. It focuses on streamlining non-essential activities while simultaneously recognizing your strengths and finding more time to spend on productive activities. Many of the techniques are applicable to life in the studio.

You'll find that owning and operating a studio presents the same challenges and obstacles faced by other business owners. On the bright side, I promise that if you keep an open mind and a focused ear, you can build greater and greater success by paying attention to, and learning, the techniques of other successful business owners. Owning a successful recording studio is a noble, exciting, and rewarding vocation. Books like the ones I have recommended here will help you keep a positive and fresh approach to that vocation.

6. Online Resources

www.artistPRO.com

An excellent online source for recording industry books and a lot more.

www.musicbooks.com

Another great place to find educational materials for the recording professional.

7. Important Professional Organizations

The National Academy of Recording Arts and Sciences (NARAS)
3402 Pico Boulevard
Santa Monica, CA 90405
(310) 392-3777
www.grammy.com

NARAS is a pre-eminent group of engineers, producers, and artists interested in promoting and improving the recording industry; and they also comprise the group responsible for putting the Grammys together. It's a terrific resource for making influential contacts and keeping abreast of industry news.

The Audio Engineering Society (AES)
60 E. 42nd Street
Room 2520
New York, NY 10165-2520
(212) 661-8528
www.aes.org

The AES, now in its fifth decade, is the only professional organization dedicated to the advancement and standardization of audio technology. The group puts on two regular international conferences per year, which allow scientists, engineers, and music technology companies to display their latest products and give technical presentations on new developments. The AES library is the most extensive source for audio technology available—offering countless volumes of books, technical papers, and videocassettes to the public. Its bi-annual conventions are informative and truly exhilarating.

The Association of Professional Recording Services (APRS)

PO Box 22

Totnes, TQ9 7YZ

UK: 01803-868600

Abroad: +44-1803-868600

www.aprs.co.uk

The APRS is an association designed to promote the cause of the recording professional in the United Kingdom. While the conventions and presentations take place overseas, the technology and issues presented are universal in their application and appeal.

The National Association of Music Merchandisers (NAMM)

5790 Armada Drive

Carlsbad, CA 92008

(760) 438-8001

www.namm.com

NAMM promotes everything to do with music technology and equipment. You name it, NAMM covers it. Guitars, recording devices, consoles, tubas, amplifiers, and music-related publications are just a few of the topics you can learn about through this organization. They offer some great online courses and present two annual conventions where members and visitors can see the latest music technology the world has to offer

B Overcoming Roadblocks: How to Avoid Being Your Own Worst Enemy

So here we go! You have found space for your studio, purchased and installed equipment, placed flyers all over town, scheduled clients, and are primed for action. What's next? Studio life is a little crazy and very unpredictable. Malfunctioning equipment, bounced checks, problems with your clients' spouses, air conditioning failure, lost manuscripts, coffee-drenched lyric sheets, band member arguments, and missed appointments are only a few of the many wonderful bumps in the road you are likely to experience on your drive down studio lane. I hope that if you've followed my guide, you'll be better prepared to handle challenges when they arise.

Unfortunately, most studio owners find that mental stagnation will eventually set in. Things will be going along famously and then—wham! Before you know what hit you, business will be slow, and you'll feel that you've run out of techniques and ideas for bringing in new clients. Worse, you're likely to experience periods when you'll lose enthusiasm and self-confidence in your ability to run your business. This phenomenon is common; don't beat yourself up if you feel down from time to time.

Recognizing that these feelings are normal is the first step in being able to overcome them. Just as we prepare ourselves for technical difficulties in the studio, we need to prepare for the occasional mental and emotional difficulties that challenge all business owners. Keep reading the trade journals, talk to other local studio owners, and attend industry seminars, which will help you to develop your technical skills. Also make sure you are taking measures to maintain your personal awareness and self-image skills..

Seminars

One of the best ways to keep your creativity alive and your motivation soaring is to learn from the motivational professionals that specialize in helping others achieve success. Large corporations have known this secret for years, and regularly employ these types of programs to keep sales and marketing forces razor sharp. If you are not familiar with motivational speakers, check them out. There is no better remedy for a slumping attitude than an infusion of creative energy.

These seminars are a great place to make new contacts, discover fresh ideas, and to have a little fun in the process. The fact that Uncle Sam will pay for the excursion (another tax-deductible business expense) makes it even more fun.

I have always made it a point to attend at least one such seminar per year; I plan for and consider them a regular part of my business development. Simply getting away from the studio and focusing my mind on other things in itself proves to be a great mental rejuvenator, and the actual seminars always inspire me to get back home and apply newly learned skills.

The following is short list of some of my favorite self-improvement seminars and books; but keep your eyes and ears open for others that may prove inspiring:

1. Motivational Speakers / Seminar Leaders

Tony Robbins

(800) 898-8669.

www.tonyrobins.com

As far as having a reputation for helping others to build success, Tony is without peer. His clients include pro athletes, movie stars, musicians, and Fortune 500 CEOs. This guy is a firecracker.

Tommy Volinchak, Tuneman Productions

101 Riverview Drive

Suite 101

Memphis, TN 38103.

www.tunemanproductions.com.

Offers seminars on "Studio Growth and Development," and "Building Success in the Music Industry." Private coaching is also available.

Zig Zigler

2009 Chenault

Suite 100

Carrollton, TX 75006

(972) 223-9191

www.zigzigler.com

Mr. Zigler is, in my opinion, the foremost expert at helping people to sell themselves. His seminars provide great insight into why successful people are successful. He does a great job of pointing out common mistakes in our personal communication styles that can lead to failure.

A Closing Note

Owning and operating a studio presents the same challenges and obstacles faced by other businesses. Greater success will be yours once you begin paying attention to and learning the techniques of other successful business people. When you get right down to it, the same kind of hard work and clever sales techniques that made McDonald's famous will also work in the recording industry. Imitate successful people and success will follow you. Try it; it works!

As I've said before, striving to be a successful recording studio owner is noble, exciting, and rewarding . Here's hoping that your studio thrives and provides you with everything you ever dreamed it would.

About the Author

Tom Volinchak is a music business veteran whose numerous industry-specific articles have appeared in publications such as *Home Recording Magazine*, *Recording Magazine*, and Nashville's newspaper, *The Tennessean*, to name a few. As the builder, owner, and operator of multiple studios, such as his 48-track digital venture, Tommy's Tunes Productions, Tom's production credits include projects with gold-record-caliber composers and artists.

After completing his B.S. in biology from Youngstown State University, Tom earned an M.B.A. in Finance. He then spent the next sixteen years in executive-level sales management and marketing positions, all within the chemicals industry, where he also provided sales training for companies such as BF Goodrich and Culligan. Having realized that his business experience could be successfully transferred to a more personally appealing field, Tom officially entered the music industry as a licensing executive for BMI-Nashville. In addition, he became an artist development executive for the Christian Country Music Association (CCMA); was a technical writer for Power Source magazine; promoted his own band, Corporate Culture, for which he acquired guest appearances on the CNBC, CNN, and Fox networks; and served for seven years as the Regional Coordinator for the Nashville Songwriters Association, wherein he was recognized for his crucial efforts to combat the Senate legislation considered detrimental to composers and artists (Sennsenbrenner Amendment).

Tom currently resides in Memphis, Tennessee, where, in addition to his own studio work, he serves as a private studio consultant, seminar host, and motivational speaker within the music industry community.

Visit Tom's website at www.tunemanproductions.com,

or email him at Tommy Tuneman@aol.com, or Tom@TunemanProductions.com.

AUDIO TECHNOLOGY BOOKS

FROM HAL LEONARD

Mackie Compact Mixers – Revised

Mackie Compact Mixers takes the mystery out of using your mixer. Written in a clear, musician-friendly style, this book will help you get the most from your small mixer, whatever its brand or model. Provides specific information and hook-up examples on Mackie's most popular models, including the "classic" 1202 and 1604 as well as the new 1202-, 1402-, 1604-VLZs, VLZ Pro and other models. Written by the author of *Live Sound for Musicians* and authorized by Mackie, this book explains the fundamental concepts of how mixing boards work, emphasizing how audio gets into and out of a mixer. Armed with this understanding of signal flow, you will be equipped to begin answering your own questions about how to set up and operate your mixer to best meet your needs.

00330477 ....$27.95

The Recording Guitarist

A Guide for Home and Studio by Jon Chappell

This is a practical, hands-on guide to a variety of recording environments, from modest home studios – where the guitarist must also act as the engineer and producer – to professional facilities outfitted with top-quality gear and staffed with audio engineers. This book will prepare guitarists for any recording situation and will help them become familiar with all facets of recording technology and procedure. Topics covered include: guitars and amps for recording; effects; mixer logic and routing strategies; synching music to moving images; and how to look and sound professional, with advice from Alex Lifeson, Carl Verheyen, Steve Lukather, Eric Johnson and others. Also includes complete info on the classic set-ups of 14 guitar greats, from Hendrix to Vai.

00330335 ....$19.95

Audio Made Easy – 2nd Edition

Audio Made Easy is a book about professional audio written in terms that everyone can understand. Chapters include info on mixers, microphones, amplifiers, speakers and how they all work together. New edition features a new section on wireless mics.

00330260 ....$12.95

Yamaha Guide to Sound Systems for Worship

The Yamaha Guide to Sound Systems for Worship is written to assist in the design, purchase, and operation of a sound system. It provides the basic information on sound systems that is most needed by ministers, members of Boards of Trustees and worship and music committees, interested members of congregations, and even employees of musical instrument dealers that sell sound systems. To be of greatest value to all, it is written to be both nondenominational and "non-brand-name."

00290243 ....$24.95

Live Sound for Musicians

Finally, a live sound book written for musicians, not engineers! *Live Sound for Musicians* tells you everything you need to know to keep your band's PA system working smoothly, from set-up to sound check right through performance. Author Rudy Trubitt give you all the information you need, and leaves out the unnecessary propeller-head details that would just slow you down. So if you're the player in the band who sets up the PA, this is the book you've been waiting for!

00330249 ....$19.95

Sound Check – The Basics of Sound and Sound Systems

Sound Check is a simplified guide to what can be a tricky subject: getting good sound. Starting with an easy-to-understand explanation of the principles and physics of sound, *Sound Check* goes on to cover amplifiers, speaker hookup, matching speakers with amps, sound reinforcement, mixers, monitor systems, grounding, and more.

00330118 ....$14.95

Yamaha Sound Reinforcement Handbook – 2nd Edition

Sound reinforcement is the use of audio amplification systems. This book is the first and only book of its kind to cover all aspects of designing and using such systems for public address and musical performance. The book features information on both the audio theory involved and the practical applications of that theory, explaining everything from microphones to loud speakers. This revised edition features almost 40 new pages and is even easier to follow with the addition of an index and a simplified page and chapter numbering system. New topics covered include: MIDI, synchronization, and an appendix on logarithms.

00500964 ....$34.95

1102